STRENGT
TRAININC

by Max Jones
(National Athletics Coach)

Weight Training for Athletics (Oscar State)	1955
Strength Training for Athletics (Ron Pickering)	1965
Second Edition	1968
Reprinted	1972, 1975
Strength Training for Athletics (Frank Dick, Carl Johnson, Wilf Paish)	1978
Strength Training (Max Jones)	1990

ISBN 0 85134 097 0   3M/29M/1090

About the Author

Prior to becoming a BAAB National Athletics Coach in 1981, Max Jones coached weightlifting as well as athletics. His squad included John Alderson who set British Powerlifting records (110kg and heavyweight) and won a bronze medal in the World Powerlifting Championships.

Since 1982 Max has been the Chief Coach for Throws and Combined Events and was a Team Coach to the Great Britain teams at the 1984 and 1988 Olympic Games.

The author acknowledges with thanks the assistance of Athletics Weekly magazine and Ernie Williams (drawings) and of Powersport International (photographs).

Designed, typeset in Times Roman and printed on 115 gsm Fineblade Cartridge by Reedprint Limited, Windsor, Berkshire, England.

CONTENTS

ATHLETICS COACH

The Coaching Journal of the B.A.A.B.

Published:
March, June, September, December

Details from:
B.A.A.B. Coaching Office,
Edgbaston House,
3 Duchess Place,
Birmingham B16 8NM

INTRODUCTION

The lifting of weights, whatever their size and shape, must be one of the oldest forms of sport known to man. Indeed most, if not all, civilisations have their legends associated with feats of strength.

Perhaps the most famous strong-man in history was the Milo of Crotona (Italy). Although many different feats have been attributed to him, perhaps his best known performance was that of carrying a four-year-old bull on his shoulders the length of the stadium (200m) at Olympia. It is calculated that

the bull weighed over 400kg and that Milo trained by lifting and carrying the bull daily until it was four years old (progressive resistance training). Milo's well developed strength undoubtedly helped him maintain a 24 year winning streak at Olympian, Pythian, Nemean and Isthmian Games.

Weight-lifting was one of the original sports included in the modern Olympics (1896) and adopted its modern form in 1928 when athletes completed three lifts — the press, the snatch and the jerk. In 1972 the press was omitted from the competition lifts. Weight-lifting's sister sport of Powerlifting has a more recent history, having only achieved championship status in the 1960's and 70's. It is now standardised at three lifts — the bench press,

Fig. 1 Milo and his improvised barbell!!

squat and the dead lift. It has become more popular (numerically) than Olympic weight-lifting, probably due to the fact that it is closely associated with body building.

Weight-training was only accepted as an integral part of the sport in the late 1950's and even then sceptics were numerous and vocal. Pre-war (1939-45) it is difficult to find examples of athletes who practised systematic strength training, probably due to the fact that natural ability and just a little training were sufficient to win.

Probably the first recorded connection between weight-lifting and athletics was in the 1870's when W.B. Curtis (Hammer) and H.E. Buermeyer (Shot) both won USA titles and were at the same time competitive weight-lifters. Little or no notice was given to this link between strength and performance.

A further glimpse of the benefits of weight-training was seen at the 1936 Olympics when the German team incorporated such training in their build up. The shot putt winner, Hans Woellke (16.20m), placed great emphasis upon barbell training.

The heavily built Les Steers (USA) broke the world record in the High Jump three times in 1941 (best 2.11m) and he may have been the first athlete to go into print on the benefits of barbell training:-

"You need strong leg muscles in the high jump, particularly when you weigh as much as I do. Only weight-lifting could have given me that extra power I need so much."

Steers was followed by Olympic gold medallists Mal Whitfield (USA — 800m), Bob Richards (USA — Pole Vault) and Parry O'Brien (USA — Shot) who between them collected six gold medals between 1948 and 1956. The one thing they all had in common is that they all used weights. O'Brien in particular attracted a lot of media coverage with his technical innovation and his dependence upon heavy progressive weight-training.

Up to the 1950's coaches had as a body been against the use of weights and the 'muscle bound' myth was exploited to great effect. But gradually more and more coaches saw with their own eyes that a systematic programme was of positive benefit to athletes. Coaches such as Geoff Dyson, Percy Cerutty and Franz Stampfl openly declared their belief in barbell training. Stampfl was quoted in a Melbourne paper as saying:-

> "Muscular strength is the determining factor, particularly in all movements where explosive speed and perfect balance are vital to first rate performances. Weight-training should be part and parcel of the training programme of every athlete."

The acceptance of weight-training as a training aid in Great Britain was underlined when in 1955 the Amateur Athletic Association published a book on strength training under the authorship of Oscar State which dealt basically with lifting techniques. Since this publication, the world of strength training has become very sophisticated and a second, third and now a fourth publication have proved necessary to keep pace with the strength needs of the modern athlete.

Chapter 1

THEORY AND DEFINITIONS

MUSCLE

The human body has three types of muscles:- smooth voluntary muscle, e.g. walls of blood vessels, cardiac muscle (the heart) and skeletal muscle, of which the latter is the prime target of the strength trainer.

Skeletal muscle is surrounded by a layer of connective tissue which provides a surface against which the surrounding muscles can glide. The muscles are composed of long thin bundles of muscle cells (fasciculus) which are groups of cells running parallel to one another to form fibre-like structures.

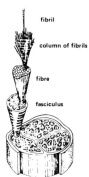

Fig. 2 (from Payne 1981)

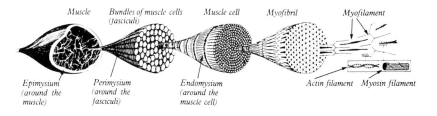

Fig. 3 (from Wirhed 1984)

The muscle cell is seen to be composed of small components called muscle fibrils or myofibrils. Myofibrils are chains of protein molecules lying in parallel which give the muscle cell a striated or striped appearance. This is due to the presence of two types of myofilament, namely actin (thinner and lighter in appearance) and myosin (thicker and darker). When the muscle contracts, the actin filaments move between the myosin filaments. As a result the myofibrils shorten and thicken.

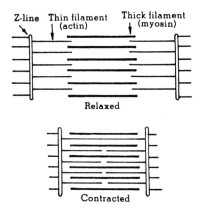

Fig. 4

3

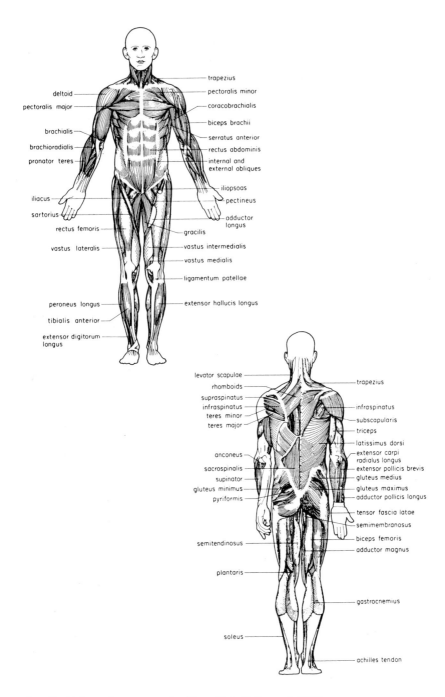

Fig. 5 Major voluntary muscles (from B & G Tancred 1984)

4

The muscle contraction is activated by the brain sending signals to the muscle fibres through the central nervous system (CNS). Each muscle is fed by motor units which are the functional units of muscular activity under neural control. Each muscle fibre is innervated by at least one motor neurone (a motor unit is a motor neurone and the muscle fibres it innervates). All of the muscle fibres within one motor unit contract or none of them contract (all-or-none law). The magnitude of the force exerted depends upon the number of fibres employed and the number of motor units recruited.

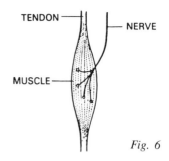

Fig. 6

There appears to be a very large learning component in one's ability to generate maximum nervous impulse instantaneously. The greater the nervous impulse, the greater will be the number of contracting motor units. If a muscle is compelled to contract with a certain force, the work is carried out by a certain number of motor units. If the force of contraction is to increase, more motor units have to be engaged. It is always the same motor units that are used for coping with a light load, and it is always the same units that thereafter are engaged when the load is increased. Obviously if we want to train the entire muscle, it must be subjected to maximal stress. Increasing strength depends partly on supplying nerve impulses of sufficient intensity to recruit the maximum number of muscle fibres.

There are two different types of muscle cell dividing the fibres into fast twitch (white, Type II) and slow twitch (red, Type I) fibres. The slow twitch (ST) fibres are better adapted to perform aerobic work, and the fast twitch (FT) anaerobic work.

Characteristics

Slow twitch fibres (Type I)

- Supplied with energy via oxygen in the blood.
- Aerobic work, e.g. long endurance activities.
- Cannot be made faster.

Fast twitch fibres (Type II)

- Supplied mainly with energy stored in the muscle (as glucose) which can be transformed into mechanical energy without oxygen.
- Anaerobic work, e.g. short sprint, heavy weight-lifting.
- Easily fatigued.
- Greater capacity to increase in size.
- 'Twitch' more frequently per second.

The percentage of each type of fibre varies from person to person with an Olympic marathon runner maybe having 90 per cent ST, whereas 'Mr. Average' would perhaps have 50 per cent of both types. In one body, different muscles would have different compositions of fibre types. The Type II fibre can be further sub-divided into IIa and IIb with the former being, through training, able to be closely associated with Type I fibres.

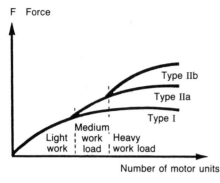

F Force

Type IIb

Type IIa

Type I

Light work | Medium work load | Heavy work load

Number of motor units

Fig. 7 (from Wirhed 1984)

The order of fibre type recruitment is more or less constant. Fast twitch motor units (individual motor units do not supply both fibre types) are the last to be activated in a muscular contraction. When a light weight is lifted slowly the vast majority of fibres used are slow twitch fibres, and when weight is added or the weight is lifted faster, additional fast twitch fibres (IIa) are recruited and at higher intensities fibres IIb. The order of recruitment is therefore ST(I) → FT(IIa) → FT(IIb), with the determining factor of whether to recruit FT motor units being the total amount of force necessary to perform the muscular contraction. This recruitment procedure means that ST motor units are predominantly recruited to perform low intensity, long-duration endurance activities.

The order of recruitment of motor units is very significant for athletes, for in events where strength and power are sought after and therefore FT fibre development is essential, performing lifts using light weights easily will not develop FT muscle fibres.

WHAT IS STRENGTH?

Strength is not easily defined, and the common definition of 'the ability to express force' is not precise enough. The strength needed to break away on the last lap of a 10,000 metres differs from the strength needed to lift a 200kg barbell, and from the strength needed to explode from the blocks in a 100 metres race. Thus much more specific sub-classifications of strength are necessary. These follow:-

Maximum Strength (absolute, gross)

This can be defined as 'the greatest force that is possible in a single maximum voluntary contraction'. It involves neither speed nor endurance factors. A slow heavy dead lift is an example of an exercise demanding maximum strength. The highest maximum values of strength are needed for those sports in which exceptional external resistance has to be overcome, e.g. weight-lifting, wrestling, arm wrestling, etc.

In athletics, maximum strength plays an important role in events such as the shot and hammer where the 7.26kg implement offers great resistance. It is possible, of course, to combine demands for maximum strength with a high speed of contraction, as for example in hammer, shot putt and discus; or with high demands on endurance, as for example in the 800 metres. The smaller the resistance to be overcome, the less the involvement of maximum strength. In sprinting, or jumping, the act of propelling the body forwards/upwards represents a great resistance to overcome and therefore the demands for maximum strength are high. The need is less in the endurance events and each athlete's event obviously has its own individual demand placed upon the component of maximum strength.

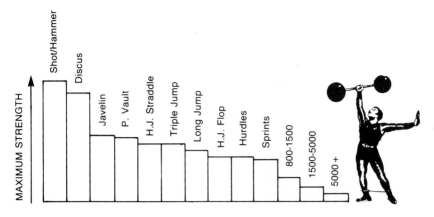

Fig. 8 Maximum strength

Elastic Strength (explosive, power, fast-strength)

This is defined as the ability of the neuro-muscular system to overcome resistance with a high speed of contraction. Both the contractile and elastic components of the muscle are assisted by reflex contraction in the expression of strength at speed. Implied is a rapid loading, which the skeletal-lever system accepts and expels at a high velocity, via a co-ordination of motor units, reflexes, elastic component and contractile component of muscle. The adjective 'elastic' is very appropriate and a key to avoiding confusion between 'speed of contraction' and 'strength of contraction'. Although this mechanism involves both of these abilities, it is their complex co-ordination and the involvement of reflexes and elastic component which identifies it as a most specific area of strength. This ability to overcome resistances with a high speed of contraction is relevant to almost every event and the majority of sports — a jump, a throw or a sprint start are all excellent examples of activities where elastic strength is required.

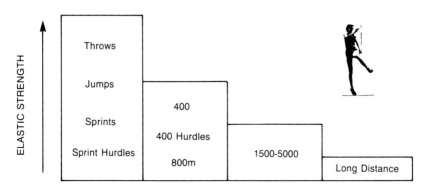

Fig. 9

7

The elastic strength of a thrower

Strength Endurance

This is the capacity of the whole organism to withstand fatigue under a long-lasting expenditure of strength. Consequently it is characterised by a relatively long duration expression of strength together with a faculty to persevere. It is an important component in events involving lactic anaerobic endurance, and also in activities such as multiple squat thrusts, sit-ups and press-ups. Obviously this ability is needed in events such as the 800 metres, but the shot putter also needs strength endurance in order to enable him to undertake an extensive weight-lifting schedule, or to reproduce 40 quality throws in a training session. It is therefore necessary in all athletic events.

Strength endurance determines performance principally in those events in which considerable resistance is to be overcome for a fairly long period of time. Thus somewhere between 400m and 3000 metres steeplechase, we would expect to find strength endurance a critical factor in performance.

Obviously an athlete will have to incorporate all these strength elements into his schedule although the emphasis given to each quality will vary from event to event, with the needs of the 1500 metre runner being different to those of the hammer thrower.

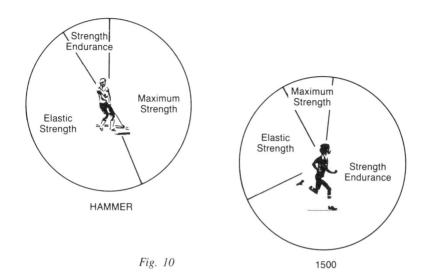

Fig. 10   1500

MUSCULAR ACTIVITY

The three different classifications of strength defined above must be given close attention during training and the planning of training. The coach must also take into consideration differing types of muscular activity when setting his schedule. These fall broadly into three sub-classes. All play a part in every athletic event, although as with the classifications of strength, the coach must be acutely aware of the exact role that each type plays in a particular event. The types are:-

Static (isometric)

Involves muscle tensions, which do not result in the muscle changing length. The muscle does not generate enough force against the mass to cause movement. Isometrics is a type of resistance training which is normally performed against an immovable object such as a wall, door frame, barbell or weight stack all loaded beyond the athlete's lifting strength. Isometrics gained rapid popularity in the 1950's and 60's based on the research performed by Hettinger and Muller (1953) which concluded that strength gains of 5% per week could be gained without high volume training. Subsequent research has down-graded these findings to a figure substantially less than 5%. If one looks at the improvement in concentric or eccentric strength, the percentage gains are considerably less than were first claimed.

Static strength is of some value to all athletes since, for example, the high jumper and the hammer thrower need static strength to maintain posture when performing their particular skills, in which force expressed by the athlete must be equal to, and balance, the force being expressed by the resistance. Lack of static strength will cause a breakdown of technique, especially when the speed of the movement is increased.

Fig. 11 gives a schematic representation of what is happening inside a muscle during isometric activity.

9

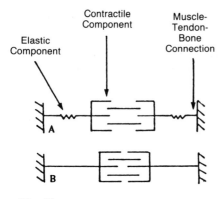

Elastic Component

Contractile Component

Muscle-Tendon-Bone Connection

A

B

Fig. 11

The kinetic energy required to pull the body's levers, and so express the force necessary in a given movement, is generated in the contractile component of muscle. This is connected, both in parallel and in series, to the elastic component which in turn is connected to the body levers. Where contraction is isometric, the levers linked by a given system do not move. This is due to a delicate process of contractile component pulling on the elastic component, the other ends of the system being fixed. Hence A – B.

During isometric muscular activity the force expressed by the athlete will obviously equal the force being expressed by the resistance. In other words, the greater the resistance, the greater will be the amount of strength required by the athlete to maintain the relationship between levers at a given joint. This implies an ultimate maximum for a given athlete in a given joint action. When the resistance exceeds the maximum the muscular activity is no longer isometric, but a type of eccentric activity.

Dynamic

Takes place when the force expressed by the athlete does not equal that imposed by the resistance and the origin and insertion of a muscle are forcefully affected by changes in muscle length. In athletic events it is this type of activity which dominates. Dynamic muscular activity is divided into overcoming (concentric) strength and yielding (eccentric strength). Take for example the bench press exercise (Fig. 12).

CONCENTRIC   ECCENTRIC

Fig. 12

With the bar on the athlete's chest, the athlete expresses force which is greater than the resistance (the barbell) causing the muscle to shorten, pulling the levers it connects towards each other, and causing the bar to rise (concentric muscular activity). After completion of the lift, some muscles will lengthen, while lowering the bar, in order to control the momentum (eccentric muscular activity). All conventional weight-training exercises exhibit both types of muscular activity. Concentric work, where the origin and insertion of the muscle move towards each other, is easily arranged and a vast range of activities are available from which athletes can select those most suitable to their needs. If we consider each athletic event, it is clear that this type of activity is that which is found most frequently. It is equally clear that by simply developing the ability to perform such activities which require a greater expression of strength (e.g. bench press) may not necessarily lead to improved performance of a given athletic event. The co-ordination and role of each joint action must be considered as a whole — and that 'whole' must be developed.

Eccentric (negative resistance)

This type of muscular activity, where force is exerted while the origin and insertion are receding from each other, falls into two sub-groups:-

Elastic Eccentric — work in which the resistance is less than the resistance which the athlete can express (e.g. the 'give' on landing in the triple jump). This strength requirement has been recognised as extremely important to athletics and training methods such as 'depth jumping' have arisen specifically to develop this quality.

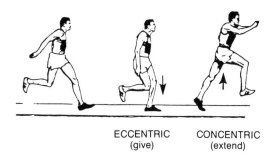

Fig. 13

ECCENTRIC (give)   CONCENTRIC (extend)

Plastic Eccentric — work in which the resistance is greater than the athlete's maximum isometric strength at any point in the range of the movement. Greater tensions can be developed during eccentric contractions (Komi 1972, Rogers & Berger 1974) and therefore eccentric training may be the most effective mechanism for stimulating adaptation within the muscle (Komi & Buskirk 1972).

There are disadvantages associated with eccentric training since the large forces developed increase the risk of muscle injury, and the exercises tend to be rather hazardous. They should only be attempted by the most experienced of weight trainers, and complex safety and 'return' arrangements are often necessary. A further disadvantage of eccentric training is the development of greater post exercise soreness than that which accompanies other forms of resistance training (Fleck & Schutt 1985).

11

Chapter 2

DEVELOPING STRENGTH

When looking for the best method of strength development athletes/coaches often refer to the numerous studies undertaken in the strength field. It is unfortunate that almost all studies thus far undertaken are with either the novice or the non-specialist college man or woman over a short time period. One must, therefore, be careful not to give total credibility to strength research when looking for guidelines for training the elite athlete. What may work for a novice athlete may not bring about the same improvements with the mature athlete who is much nearer his genetic potential. It is important that the coach/athlete takes heed of both the empirical knowledge built up over many years by coaches working with athletes and the results of research studies.

MAXIMUM STRENGTH DEVELOPMENT

To gain any type of strength it is necessary to work consistently hard. To make significant gains in the area of maximum strength some work must be made near to failure. This means that at the end of a set the muscles were performing a voluntary maximal contraction.

Early research work undertaken by Berger (1962a and 1962b) indicated that the optimum number of sets and repetitions was 3 sets of 6 repetitions (3 × 6). In later studies Berger (1963) also found significant gains with other combinations of sets and repetitions. Subsequent studies have indicated that maximal strength is best accomplished by using loads representing 70%-100% of maximum (1-12 repetitions maximum (RM)), and Viitasalo et al (1981) suggested that increases in maximal strength occur with sets of no more than 8 repetitions. It appears that to develop maximum strength not only are high loads required, but also the duration of this stimulus appears to be important and subsequently many studies recommend repetitions in the 4-8 repetition range. Schmidtbleicher (1986) states that an athlete reaches his strength potential faster if he/she initially works for the development of muscle mass, followed at a later stage by lower repetitions which favour muscle recruitment and nervous system training. The best means of increasing muscular cross section (hypertrophy) appears to be in the range of 6-12 repetitions, hence the many examples of elite bodybuilders who acquire high maximum strength whilst working for increased muscle mass. Maughan (1986) also states that the most important factor in determining a muscle's strength is its size — the cross-sectional area of the whole muscle.

It therefore seems that for the novice athlete high repetitions would appear to coincide with the best method of gaining both strength, muscle and the opportunity to acquire lifting skills through multiple repetition of the movement.

Using lower repetitions (1-5) and higher intensity (85%-100%) will also increase maximum strength. With this regime gains are made via the nervous system and better muscle recruitment. The advantage of using low repetitions is that only minimal hypertrophy occurs, which is a positive advantage for those athletes who must have a high strength to bodyweight ratio. When training for increased maximum strength it is important to ensure that adequate recovery periods of up to 5 minutes are taken between sets to avoid cumulative fatigue.

Number of repetitions	No. of sets	Recovery time	Evaluation procedure
Hypertrophy 6-12 repetitions	5 – 6	3 mins	Maximum lifts
Muscle Recruitment 1-5 repetitions	5 – 8	5 mins	Dynamometer test

Fig. 14 Maximum strength.

ELASTIC STRENGTH

Elastic strength, according to Dick (1989), can be developed by improving maximum strength and/or speed of co-ordinated muscle contraction, but carries with it the problem of effecting an optimal compromise of development that can be translated to the sports technique. The problem, as seen by Dick, is because if the athlete works with a heavy loading then both strength and speed of contraction will develop for that specific exercise.

Harre (1973) believes that elastic strength is best brought about by the following regime:-

75% loading × 4-6 sets × 6-10 repetitions
with 5 minutes recovery between sets.

Whereas with maximum strength regimes the athlete would work to the point of failure, a low loading would fall short of this state of fatigue. To acquire elastic strength the athlete must concentrate upon the quality of the movement with the selected loading allowing quick/explosive repetitions. Deep concentration is necessary to ensure muscle recruitment and explosive movement.

It is unwise to try to develop elastic strength in isolation. The aim should be to develop such strength in parallel with gains in maximum strength.

A very effective way of making significant strength gains in both elastic and maximum strength is by super-setting a maximum strength activity (@ 85-100%) with an elastic strength exercise (@ 55-60%). This super-setting of exercises should be programmed with discretion and should not exceed blocks of work lasting 3-4 weeks.

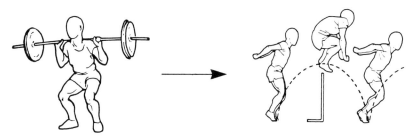

Fig. 15 Maximum elastic super sets — i.e. a set of 6 repetitions squatting is immediately followed by five consecutive jumps over hurdles. Five minutes rest, then repeat.

13

Elastic strength exercises are sometimes more easily and probably more beneficially performed away from formal barbell exercises, i.e. with weighted jackets, gymnastics, bounding, medicine ball work etc. When working for elastic strength always ensure that adequate recovery is allowed so that fatigue does not interfere with the execution of the exercise.

Number of repetitions	No. of sets	Recovery time	Evaluation procedure
6-10 repetitions	4 – 6	5 mins	Bounding and Jumping tests

Fig. 16 Elastic strength.

STRENGTH ENDURANCE

In all athletics events strength endurance will have a part to play, e.g. the shot putter will have to spend long training sessions both throwing and lifting weights which will require strength endurance.

It would appear that the foundation of training in strength endurance lies in the ability to perform the highest possible number of repetitions against a loading which is greater than that normally experienced in the event.

Strength endurance exercises are many and varied and break down into two groups:-

Event specific — running in snow, uphill, through sand, dragging a weight, wearing weighted jacket, etc.

General — using general exercises in the form of a circuit, i.e. repetitions of approximately 50-70% of maximum, with a loading of 40-60% maximum and optimal recovery between, seems a sound rule of thumb.

To develop the strength endurance factor it is necessary to use high repetitions. Recommendations vary as to the precise number of sets and repetitions that are to be used. A summary of research conducted seems to indicate that it is necessary to use 10-30 repetitions with a loading of 30-60% of maximum, with a short rest in between sets of 30 to 120 seconds. These figures give wide scope for the athlete/coach to construct a circuit or stage training programme.

Thus using lighter loads and repeating an exercise to the point of fatigue will also improve maximum strength, but to a very limited extent, as such work moves into an area of endurance training. For the young athlete this type of work over many exercises will establish a general basis of strength.

Number of repetitions	No. of sets	Recovery time	Evaluation procedure
25%-50% of maximum (circuits)	4 – 6	optimal	Maximum repetitions
			Maximum holding time

Fig. 17 Strength endurance.

ECCENTRIC STRENGTH

Eccentric training refers to a muscular contraction in which the muscle lengthens. Such eccentric contractions take place on normal concentric work, i.e. when the weight is lowered after the weight has been lifted. The lifting of a weight causes the muscle to shorten as it contracts (concentric contraction) and to lengthen as the weight is lowered (eccentric contraction). Eccentric contraction training can be divided into two types:-

Elastic eccentric work — here the resistance may be less than the maximum strength which the athlete can express. An example of this movement can be seen in the acceptance of body momentum as the athlete moves into the basic shot throw position (Fig. 18) or with each landing/take-off in triple jumping. The need to develop an athlete's ability to perform such muscular activity has given rise to training methods such as depth jumping.

Fig. 18

Plastic eccentric work — here the resistance imposed is greater than the athlete's maximum isometric strength at any point in the range of movement. Thus the athlete can only attempt to control the losing struggle he has with the resistance. An athlete who may be able to bench press a 100kg barbell may well be able to use a 120kg barbell when resisting against the lowering of the barbell.

Because of the greater amount of resistance during eccentric training the muscle tension is higher than it is during isometric or concentric contractions (Olson, Schmidt & Johnson 1972). This increased muscle tension has led to many advocating eccentric training as the best method of increasing strength. The dangers inherent in such methods are however apparent and may suggest that they should be avoided except for the most experienced and mature athletes.

The optimum resistance to be used for eccentric training appears to be in the area of 120% of maximum (IRM) (Johnson, Adamczy, Tennoe & Stromme 1976):

Number of repetitions	No. of sets	Recovery time	Evaluation procedure
1-5	4 – 6	5 mins	Maximum lifts

Fig. 19 Eccentric strength.

ISOMETRICS

Isometric or static resistance training refers to a muscular contraction where no change in the length of muscle takes place. Isometric training normally takes place against an immovable object. In the early fifties claims were made that substantial strength gains could be made by one daily two-thirds of maximal isometric contraction of six seconds duration (Hettinger & Muller

1953). Subsequent research (i.e. Fleck & Schutt 1985) indicated that strength gains of this magnitude were doubtful. It does not follow that isometric exercises will develop other types of strength by the same margin (Brunner 1967).

In athletics it is probably best to use strength training that corresponds to the type of contraction used in the event's technique and obviously concentric work would be of greater benefit to the athlete.

An area where isometric work can be of great benefit is in the maintenance of posture, e.g. the torso in the long jump take-off or in the shot glide. Simple exercises such as double-footed bounds whilst holding a medicine ball outstretched will help to develop postural strength. Isometric work as advanced by Hettinger & Muller has limited practical application to the dynamic sport of athletics.

Number of repetitions	No. of sets	Recovery time	Evaluation procedure
3-10 secs. duration	3 – 10	short	Dynomometer

Fig. 20

ISOKINETICS

Isokinetics refers to a muscular contraction performed at a constant angular limb velocity and, unlike other types of resistance training, there is no set resistance to meet; rather the velocity of movement is controlled. Using isokinetic machines the athlete is able to exert maximum force throughout the whole range of the movement. Research findings indicate that many and varied combinations of sets and repetitions of isokinetic training can cause increases in strength.

The main drawback in using isokinetic machines is that only the more expensive machines give an accurate feedback of the force generated or the actual work performed. Because of the lack of visible movement of a weight some athletes find motivation a problem.

VARIABLE RESISTANCE

Variable resistance equipment (e.g. Nautilus) through a cam or pulley arrangement alters the resistance throughout the range of motion of an exercise in an attempt to match the increases and decreases in strength throughout the range of motion of the exercise. This forces the muscle to work at maximum and produce maximum strength gains. Little research, thus far, has been performed with specialist athletes, but with non-athletes considerable strength gains have been achieved. A major drawback to 'cam' machines is their considerable cost and lack of versatility.

MACHINE vs. FREE WEIGHTS

The athlete is often faced with the choice of using either free weights or machines. The majority of elite athletes have graduated to 'free weights', although much of their early work may have been performed with machines or a combination of strength apparatus. The reasons why the simple free weight (barbell, etc.) apparatus is still popular are:-

(1) Most machine exercise units offer exercises across single joints, whereas the athlete in his event moves in multi-joints and therefore to be trained in multi-joint exercises is beneficial.

(2) Machines with restricted acceleration movements may interfere with the natural patterns of acceleration-deceleration in the muscle.

(3) Machines do not work stabilizing muscles as much because the weight is supported. The athlete does not have to control the weight so that the stability of the joint is not as good as it could be using free weights.

(4) Machines work on isolated muscle groups, whereas in athletics it is more beneficial to perform exercises where many muscle groups are involved so that all the exercised area of the body is of proportional strength.

Machines have a vital and important role in developing strength for athletics and the advantages of such machines are:-

(1) The majority of machine weight equipment is safe and easy to use. Since little technique has to be learned, it is a relatively safe method of strength training for the novice.

(2) Certain muscle groups can be worked more effectively on machines than with free weights, e.g. adductors and abductors.

(3) When rehabilitating it is possible to isolate muscle in order to 'work around' an injury. Machines perform a good job in focussing on a particular muscle area.

The choice by the athlete should not be an 'either-or' question, but really a matter of constructing a schedule that makes the best combination of both free weights and machines.

Machine/fixed path weights   *Free weights — barbell and dumbell*

BASIC PRINCIPLES WHEN CONSTRUCTING A SCHEDULE

WHICH EXERCISES?

The choice of exercises is almost limitless and can lead to confusion on the part of the coaches trying to construct a schedule. There tends to be two schools of thought on exercise selection:-

(1) *Specific school* — advocates looking at the event specific movement and trying to mirror the movement in the strength training exercise. A discus thrower, for example, would perform 'dumbell flys', lying on a 35° inclined bench in order to simulate the arm angle during the throwing movement.

(2) *General school* — advocates performing general strength exercises such as pulling, squatting, and pressing in order to raise strength levels. Specific strength would be obtained by performing event specific exercises on the track with the discus thrower, for example, throwing a heavy discus from the standing throw position.

The main argument against performing event specific exercises with barbells and dumbells is that the imitation can never be one hundred per cent and will almost certainly not duplicate the speed or the sequence of muscle recruitment that takes place in the athletics arena.

It is recommended that a mixture of general and event specific exercises be incorporated in the schedule with the aforementioned discus thrower performing both bench press for general strength and dumbell flys for event specific strength development.

EXERCISE ORDER

When the exercises have been selected they must be put into a sequence most favourable to energy expenditure. It is advisable to alternate body parts, e.g. if the first exercise is power cleaning, the next exercise should be an upper body one to give the legs/lower back the chance to recover. Exercises that require skill and co-ordination should be performed at the start of the session when the athlete is fresh and not at the very end when the athlete is exhausted. It is preferable to perform exercises that require multiple muscle groups to work, e.g. cleans, squats, etc. in the first half of the session, with the exercises that isolate muscle groups, e.g. curls, calf raises, near the end of the session. Abdominal exercises are performed last in the sequence since those muscles are required to stabilise the body in most exercises and should not be unduly fatigued until they are no longer of use.

HOW LONG BETWEEN SESSIONS?

What happens when the athlete overloads his existing strength status in a given activity has been illustrated by the Russian bio-chemist Yakovlev as in Fig. 21.

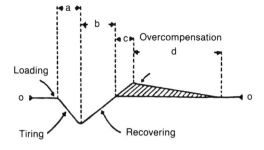

Fig. 21 Yakovlev Model of Supercompensation (from Dick, 1980, p.242)

After the sequence of loading-tiring-recovery, there exists the phenomenon of 'over-compensation'. It is clear that the athlete is able to accept an increased loading during this period of 'over-compensation' but, as can be seen from Fig. 22, the timing of the next 'loading' is quite critical — too soon (incomplete recovery) and the athlete may not make strength gains (Fig. 23b) and likewise with too long a recovery gains would be minimal.

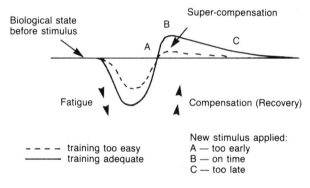

Fig. 22 Modified from NSCA Journal, Vol 8, No. 5, 1986

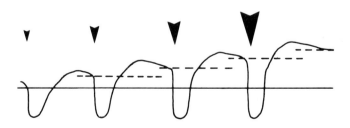

Fig. 23a Schematic representation of progressive overload based on overcompensation (from Harre, 1973)

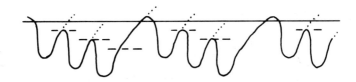

Fig. 23b Schematic representation of progressive overload based on incomplete recovery (from Harre, 1973)

By tradition the most common form of workout days is Monday-Wednesday-Friday, which allows a 48-hour recovery between sessions. Certainly for beginners this regime will provide optimum recovery and strength gains. As the athlete matures, more frequent sessions may be tolerated although it will be worth noting the following:-

(1) It is a mistake to regard all sessions as being equal in volume and in one week there should be variation (Fig. 24). When involved in heavy leg work the athlete may only be able to tolerate one or two sessions per week and therefore may need more than 48 hours to recover, whereas on exercises such as barbell curling the recovery may be adequate. In Fig. 24 the athlete would not perform leg work on the Wednesday workout.

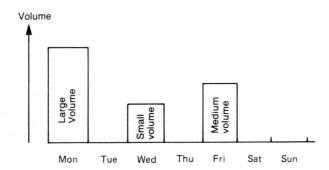

Fig. 24

The variation in volume should not only be restricted to a weekly cycle, but used on a longer period of time when light/medium/heavy volume weeks are mixed to allow optimum recovery and progression.

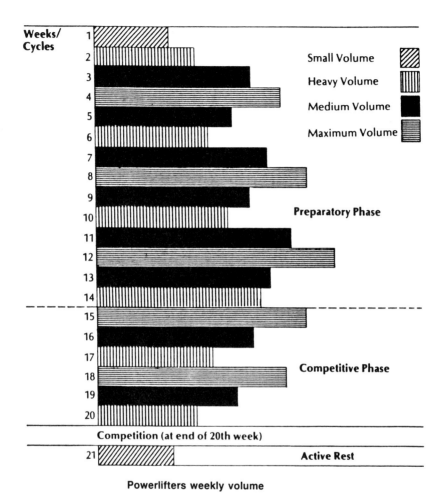

Powerlifters weekly volume

Fig. 25 Twenty-week training cycle for lifters of advanced qualification (from Lear, 1982)

HOW MUCH LOAD?

As previously discussed, the amount of resistance (load) used affects the type of strength that is acquired. When designing a strength programme the load for each repetition must be chosen.

As you move away from the strength zone (RM 1-6) the gains in strength will diminish until at the end of the scale they will be negligible. Novice athletes will make outstanding strength gains on high repetitions, e.g. 10-15, but much of this apparent gain will be from skill acquisition and enhanced muscle recruitment.

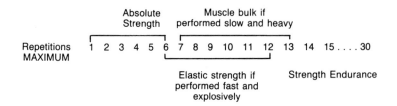

Fig. 26

When designing a resistance training schedule you can use either:-

(a) *Repetition maximums* — a load which allows an exercise movement to be performed a maximum of four times would be called the four repetition maximum (4 RM).

or

(b) *Percentages* — if an athlete has a best lift of 100kg (1 RM) an 80% load would be 80kg. Well established charts are available with predicted percentage loads from a known maximal lift. These are used to determine the load for performing a set number of repetitions. A person can look at the 1 RM or 100% load and determine a load that could be done 10 times.

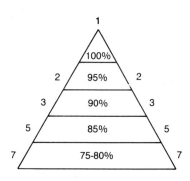

Fig. 27 Pyramid relating intensity and extent of loading, suggested by BUHRE in 'Die Lehre der Leichtathletik' 26.1.71

Conversely, a person might want to determine the 10 RM or 95% load and predict what could be done for 1 RM. It should be noted that there are individual variations and that no two athletes are exactly the same — the charts are for guidance only.

% of 1 RM	100%	95%	90%	85%	80%	75%
REPS	1	2	4	6	8	10
KG lifted	220.00	209.00	198.00	187.00	176.00	165.00
	215.00	204.25	193.50	182.75	172.00	161.25
	210.00	199.50	189.00	178.50	168.00	157.50
	205.00	194.75	184.50	174.25	164.00	153.75
	200.00	190.00	180.00	170.00	160.00	150.00
	195.00	185.25	175.50	165.75	156.00	146.25
	190.00	180.50	171.00	161.50	152.00	142.50
	185.00	175.75	166.50	157.25	148.00	138.75
	180.00	171.00	162.00	153.00	144.00	135.00
	175.00	166.25	157.50	148.75	140.00	131.25
	170.00	161.50	153.00	144.50	136.00	127.50
	165.00	156.75	148.50	140.25	132.00	123.75
	160.00	152.00	144.00	136.00	128.00	120.00
	155.00	147.25	139.50	131.75	124.00	116.25
	150.00	142.50	135.00	127.50	120.00	112.50
	145.00	137.75	130.50	123.25	116.00	108.75
	140.00	133.00	126.00	119.00	112.00	105.00
	135.00	128.25	121.50	114.75	108.00	101.25
	130.00	123.50	117.00	110.50	104.00	97.50
	125.00	118.75	112.50	106.25	100.00	93.75
	120.00	114.00	108.00	102.00	96.00	90.00
	115.00	109.25	103.50	97.75	92.00	86.25
	110.00	104.50	99.00	93.50	88.00	82.50
	105.00	99.75	94.50	89.25	84.00	78.75

Table developed by Mike Clark, Strength and Conditioning Specialist, University of Oregon.

Fig. 28   (modified from Fleck and Kraemer 1987)

HOW QUICKLY IS STRENGTH LOST?

Research indicates that strength is lost at a slower rate than it was acquired (Morehouse 1967, Waldman & Stull 1969) but such research has not yet given exact guidelines to the loadings, frequency etc. that are needed to maintain strength levels. Strength gains made during the off-season can be maintained during the competitive season by using only a fraction of the volume necessary to gain strength. To maintain strength levels the loadings (intensity) should be kept high, but the volume of weights lifted should be drastically reduced.

Volume is the quantity of work performed in a workout and usually relates to those lifts of 70% and over on one's best lifts (1 RM). A thrower who during the winter period had performed three three-hour sessions can maintain his strength with two one-hour sessions each week in summer.

The experienced athlete with an extensive background of strength training will find it relatively easy to maintain strength levels. The novice athlete must ensure that strength training is maintained during the competitive season. As can be seen in Fig. 29, athletes with a short base to the pyramid will experience rapid strength losses with the cessation of strength training.

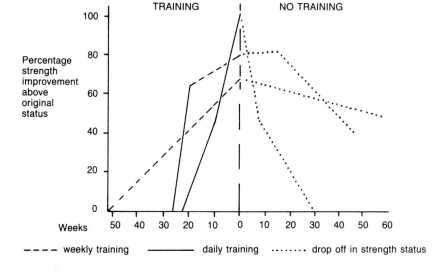

Fig. 29 Effect of weekly and daily strength training compared in terms of gain on cessation of training (from HETTINGER 1961)

Chapter 3

PLANNING

PLANNING — POST NOVICE STAGE

It is of the utmost importance that the training year is apportioned out into phases so that a competitive peak is achieved at the designed time. Before looking at the options available to the athlete in strength training, he/she must work backwards from the important competition targets of the following season. Once this basic competition programme is mapped out, the coach must divide the year into phases which will lead up to a competitive climax.

The training year can be either viewed as one whole (single periodisation) or sub-divided into two unequal segments (double periodisation) as shown below (Fig. 30a & Fig. 30b). The sub-divisions illustrated should not be taken literally since the phases will vary from athlete to athlete and from year to year.

Fig. 30a Single Periodised Year

months	Nov	Dec	Jan	Feb	Mar	Apr	May	Jun	Jul	Aug	Sep	Oct
phases	1			2				3	4		5	6
periods	preparation							competition				trans-ition

Fig. 30b Double Periodised Year

months	Nov	Dec	Jan	Feb	Mar	Apr	May	Jun	Jul	Aug	Sep	Oct
phases	1^1	2^1		3_1	1_2	2_2		3_2	4		5	6
	preparation			comp.	preparation			competition				trans-ition

Obviously any planning for strength training will have to take into account the other parts of the schedule that draw upon the same energy source and limited time allocation. With this in mind the schedule will be a compromise since the athlete must develop his differing physical requirements in a balanced way.

To achieve success at national and international levels it is essential to sub-divide the whole athletic year into a preparation phase, a competition phase and a transition phase. The long preparation phase lays a firm base for the competition phase.

The athletic year will progress gradually from general work to the specific, and from large quantities to quality; lots of general work in the depths of winter, tapering to specific, high quality, low volume work in the competitive period.

Dividing the year into phases is called periodisation. It is possible to use double periodisation or single periodisation. For athletes such as sprinters, jumpers and shot putters, double periodisation satisfies the need by having two competitive phases in the year (indoor and outdoor) and, with constant changes of emphasis, it certainly avoids both staleness and boredom.

The overriding advantage of single periodisation is that the long preparation phase ensures that a sound fitness base is achieved. An injury in the second preparation phase of a double periodised year could leave the athlete woefully short of conditioning for the summer competitive season.

Whichever periodisation option is chosen, the phases are tackled with the same principles in mind.

Early preparation phase $(1 - 1^1 - 1^2)$

Here the emphasis is on conditioning or training to train. The repetitions are high and the volume great, but the intensity is low due to minimal rest periods between sets and exercises. Circuit training would play a major role in this phase as would 'training like a body-builder' with weights – high repetitions – many exercises – short recovery. The work is of a general nature with attempt to strengthen/condition all joint actions. There is little or no need to be event specific in this phase of the training year.

Second preparation phase $(2 - 2^1 - 2^2)$

This could be termed the 'strength phase' with the volume high and intensities greatly increased over the previous phase. This is a very exhausting phase since the loads handled will be heavy. The training units will become more specific, although basic 'common core' strength movements are an integral part of the schedule. It is during this phase that the strength status of the athlete will be significantly increased.

Competition phase $(3 - 5 - 3^1 - 3^2)$

The volume and, in certain events, the frequency of strength training will be markedly reduced. The emphasis will be on quick explosive movements, adequate recuperation and an overall reduction in work load. Repetitions will be reduced and the weights chosen will be less than the repetition maximum (RM).

Mid-competitive phase (4)

It is impossible to maintain peak performances for months on end; four to five weeks is often as long as the athlete will be able to maintain a high standard of performance. To enable a second peak to be reached it is necessary to undergo a block of work that is similar to that of the preparation phase. It is a huge mistake to return to volumes undertaken in winter, but rather the athlete should return to uninterrupted training at an intensity and volume level that does not drain the athlete — 'leave the gym on your toes, not on your heels'.

Transition phase

This is a period of active recovery. Initially, at the end of the competitive season, a short rest should be taken followed by a change of exercise; swimming, soccer, basketball or squash for example. This is an important phase which recharges the batteries both physically and mentally.

Constructing a schedule

It is important to look at schedules from different development levels — what is suitable for the advanced athlete will almost certainly be unsuitable for the novice. Their capacities, skill level, motivation etc. will be totally different and therefore three broad classifications will be looked at — novice, intermediate and advanced.

NOVICE

Definition — 'Little or no experience of formal strength training'.

Before looking for strength gains there should be a period where the athlete acquires the skills of weight-training. Repetitions should be high (8-12) to ensure that the skill can be practised over and over again. There should be no loading to the point of near failure, since working with relatively heavy loads will need ingrained skill that will not break down under pressure. With this in mind there is a need for adequate rest periods between sets to ensure adequate recovery, since skills will break down in an environment of fatigue. A schedule for a novice lifter should be concerned with all-round strength development and not with event specialisation.

Novice schedule — skill learning — weeks 1-4
Schedule A

1. General warm-up
2. Power clean   — 3 sets of 8 repetitions (3 × 8)
3. Bench press   — 3 × 10
4. Back squat   — 2 × 20 (light weight — technique only emphasis)
5. Press   — 2 × 12
6. Curl   — 2 × 12
7. Pull-downs   — 2 × 15
8. Calf-raise   — 2 × 20
9. Sit-ups   — 2 × 20   *Twice per week
10. Side bends   — 2 × 10 (each side)   *Two mins. between sets

Schedule B — strength conditioning — weeks 5-12 (1st half of winter)

Sessions 1 & 2 (e.g. Monday & Wednesday)

	Warm-up	Work	Rest period
1. General warm-up			
2. Power clean	10	3 × 8	3 mins.
3. Bench press	12	3 × 10	2½mins.
4. Back squat	10	3 × 8	3 mins.
5. Press	12	3 × 10	2 mins.
6. Sit-ups	—	2 × 20	2 mins.
7. Side bends	—	2 × 10	2 mins.

Session 3 (e.g. Friday)

	Warm-up	Work	Rest period
1. General warm-up			
2. Press	10	3 × 10	2 mins.
3. Curl	12	3 × 10	1½mins.
4. Calf-raise	—	2 × 20	2 mins.

5. Pull-downs	10	2 × 10	2 mins.
6. Sit-ups		20 ⎫	
Side bends	Circuit	10 ⎬ 2 sets	2 mins
Chinnies		20 ⎭	

Schedule C — strength acquisition — weeks 13-25 (2nd half winter)

Sessions 1 & 2

1. General warm-up			
2. Power clean	10	10 − 8 − 6 − 6	3 mins.
3. Bench press	12	10 − 8 − 7 − 6	2 mins.
4. Back squat	10	4 × 8	3 mins.
5. Press	10	4 × 8	2 mins.
6. Sit-ups ⎫	Circuit	20 ⎫ 2 sets	2 mins.
Side bends ⎭		10 ⎭	

Session 3

As for Schedule C but without back squats. Reduce the weights by 10 per cent and the number of sets on each exercise by one.

Schedule D — maintenance — weeks 26 onwards (spring/summer) once per week

	Warm-up	Work	Rest period
1. General warm-up			
2. Power clean	8	2 × 6	2 mins.
3. Bench press	10	2 × 6	2 mins.
4. Back squat	10	2 × 6	2 mins.
5. Sit-ups	—	1 × 20	

For exercises 2-4 weights should be light enough to ensure that each repetition is performed with vigour and power (e.g. 90% of previous poundages).

The above schedules intentionally use only a few exercises so that the athlete is confident and skilful in the execution of the exercises. The lack of variety does not deter the novice lifter since the gains he is making are a great motivating factor.

INTERMEDIATE STAGE

Having experienced one year on a basic all-round strength programme, the next progression is to adopt a more elaborate schedule.

Preparation Phase 1 (6 weeks)

This is the 'training to train' phase where the emphasis is on conditioning the athlete in order to accept the higher loads which are to follow. The work should be a mixture of circuits and formal strength work, although the strength dividing line may well encompass jumping and running activities. It is assumed that the athlete trains once per day and up to a maximum of seven days per week.

Percentages

You will note that in the following schedules a percentage figure is given underneath the recommended sets and repetitions. These indicate the percentage of a one repetition maximum lift, so that if an athlete can lift a maximum for one repetition of 100kg, the 70 per cent figure would mean that he would lift 70kg for the number of repetitions indicated. The figures in the schedules are for guidance only to show how the athlete should progress as the schedule develops. To rely on percentages when constructing a schedule can have serious drawbacks:-

1. Just what is 100% (IRM)? An athlete's maximum lift can vary from day to day, if not from hour to hour, so that the coach can never be certain of an exact percentage.

2. Even though the relationship between IRM and sub-maximal loads has been established with a fair degree of precision, individual differences due to neural factors and fibre typing can vary greatly. For instance, while most individuals usually perform 11 to 12 repetitions at 70% of IRM, one individual might be able to manage say 13 and another only 10.

3. The percentage relationship between maximum and sub-maximal repetitions is different from one muscle to another. For example, at 60 per cent of maximum research indicates that many more repetitions can be performed at the leg press than on leg curls.

4. To try and keep pace with prescribed percentage increases is a mistake since this will vary greatly from individual to individual.

An alternative to percentage loadings is to work out training loads based on the repetitions prescribed. Three sets of six repetitions (3×6) means to the coach that the athlete should have to work very hard on the last two sets, e.g. 60kg $\times$ 6, 70kg $\times$ 6, $67\frac{1}{2}$kg $\times$ 6. The 70 $\times$ 6 should mean that 70kg $\times$ 7 is not possible and that a sixth repetition is extremely hard work, and since the muscle is therefore fatigued then the last set is also extremely hard work. With this in mind the athlete must always lift at the same intensity and on an 'off day' may use less weight but just as much energy and on a 'very good day' more weight to ensure that he is working up to overload.

Year Plan

Month	Oct	Nov		Dec		Jan	Feb	Mar	Apr	May	Jun	Jul	Aug	Sep
Phase	I		R	IIa		R	IIb			R	III	IV	V	VI
Period	PREPARATION									COMPETITION				TRAN-SITION

R = RECOVERY

Fig. 31

Aims

Phase 1. To build a base of fitness
Phase 2. To increase strength significantly
Phase 3. To maintain strength levels
Phase 4. To ensure that strength levels are 'topped up'
Phase 5. To maintain strength levels
Phase 6. Active rest.

Microcycle

Phase I — Duration 6 weeks

Days	1	2	3	4	5	6	7
Work	Strength 'A'		Strength 'B'	Strength 'A'		Strength 'B'	

Weekly details and progressions

Training unit and exercises	Warm ups	Week 1	Week 2	Week 3	Week 4	Week 5	Week 6	Week 7	Week 8	Week 9	Week 10
Strength A											
Clean	10	3 × 7 70%	3 × 7 72½%	4 × 7 72½%	3 × 8 72½%	3 × 8 75%	4 × 8 75%				
Bench press	12	3 × 10 65%	3 × 11 65%	3 × 12 65%	3 × 10 70%	3 × 11 70%	3 × 12 70%				
Back squats	10	3 × 8 70%	3 × 9 70%	3 × 10 70%	3 × 8 75%	3 × 9 75%	3 × 10 75%				
Press	10	3 × 10 65%	3 × 10 65%	3 × 10 67½%	3 × 10 70%	3 × 10 70%	3 × 10 70%				
Bent over rowing	10	2 × 10									
Laterals	10	2 × 10									
Curls	10	2 × 10									
Sit-ups		2 × 20									
Side bends		2 × 10									
Leg raises		2 × 20									
Strength B (circuit/stage training) 3 × 2 ×											
Press-ups		15	20	25	25	25	28				
E&P tuck jump		15	20	24	24	24	26				
Burpees		20	25	30	30	30	35				
Medicine ball kick		15	20	20	20	25	25				

{ Tri set (Bent over rowing, Laterals, Curls)

{ Tri set (Sit-ups, Side bends, Leg raises)

N.B. The percentage figures are those calculated at Week One — 3 × 12 at 70% would not be possible in Week One but can be achieved in Week Six due to increased strength. A test for one repetition maximum in Week Six would upgrade these percentages.

(Tri set: three exercises performed in rotation; rest, then repeat.)

Preparation Phase IIa

Here the athlete aims to increase his strength status.

Microcycle

Phase IIa — 10 weeks

Days	1	2	3	4	5	6	7
Work	Strength 'A'		Strength 'A'		Strength 'B'		

Weekly details and progressions

Training unit and exercises	Warm ups	Week 1	Week 2	Week 3	Week 4	Week 5	Week 6	Week 7	Week 8	Week 9	Week 10
Strength A											
Clean	8-6	3×6 82½%	3×6 82½%	3×7 82½%	3×7 82½%	3×6 85%	3×6 85%	3×7 85%	3×7 85%	3×6 87½%	3×6 87½%
Bench press	10-8	3×7 80%	3×10 75%	3×7 80%	3×10 75%	3×7 82½%	3×10 77½%	3×7 82½%	3×10 77½%	3×7 85%	3×10 77½%
Back squats	10	3×8 70%	3×8 72½%	3×8 75%	3×8 77½%	3×8 80%	3×8 80%	3×8 75%	3×8 80%	3×8 75%	3×8 82½%
Press	10	3×8 75%	⟶				3×8 80%	⟶			
Sit-ups		2×20 ⎱ Super set ⟶									
Side bends		2×10 ⎰									
Strength B											
Front squat	6	3×5 75% ⎱ Super set ⟶									
Drop jumps		3×5 B/W ⎰									
Bench press	10	3×5 75% ⎱ Super set ⟶									
Clap press-ups		3×5 B/W ⎰									
Technique snatches	5	3×5 60% ⎱ Super set ⟶									
Medicine ball push	5	3×5 4kg ⎰									
Sit-ups		2×30 B/W ⎱ Super set ⟶									
Leg raises		2×15 B/W ⎰									

Exercises bracketed are performed together — a conventional weight exercise followed by an explosive reflex movement.

Recovery Phase (3 weeks)

It is essential that the athlete be allowed to recover from this bout of heavy strength work. For a period of three weeks the athlete will adopt a maintenance programme where he/she will keep in touch with weights without attempting to 'strain or gain'.

Preparation Phase IIb — 10 weeks

Microcycle

Days	1	2	3	4	5	6	7
Work	Strength 'A'		Strength 'A'		Strength 'B'		

Weekly details and progressions

Training unit and exercises	Warm ups	Week 1	Week 2	Week 3	Week 4	Week 5	Week 6	Week 7	Week 8	Week 9	Week 10
Strength A											
Snatch	8	3×6 70%	3×6 70%	3×7 70%	3×7 70%	3×7 75%	3×6 75%	3×6 75%	3×7 75%	3×7 75%	3×6 77½%
Bench press	10	3×6 75%	3×6 75%	3×7 75%	3×7 75%	3×6 77½%	3×7 77½%	3×6 80%	3×6 80%	3×6 80%	3×7 80%
Back squats (day 1 only)	10	3×6 80% →			3×7 80% →			3×6 82½% →			3×7 82½%
Push press	8	3×5 70% →					3×5 75% →				
Sit-ups		3×20 ⎫ →									
Side bends (day 1 only)		2×10 ⎭									

Strength B

As for Session 'B' on preparation phase IIa but exercises changed:-

Back squat ⎫	Incline bench ⎫	Fast clean ⎫
Hurdle jumps ⎭	Incline clap press ⎭	Med. ball, o/head throw ⎭

Recovery Phase II (2 weeks)

Once again, at the end of such a long strength phase there must be 1-2 weeks of simply 'ticking over' with regards to strength work.

Competitive Season (Phases III, IV, V)

Here the aim is to maintain, not increase, strength.

Microcycle

Phase III and IV

Days	1	2	3	4	5	6	7
Work	Strength 'A'					Competition	

Weekly details and progressions

Training unit and exercises	Warm ups	Week 1	Week 2	Week 3	Week 4	Week 5	Week 6	Week 7	Week 8	Week 9	Week 10
Strength A											
Snatch	6	3 × 4 75% ────────────────▶									
Dynamic squats*	8	3 × 5 75% ────────────────▶					Length of progression depends upon the competitive demands				
Bench press (fast)	8	3 × 5 75% ────────────────▶									
Push press	6	2 × 5 75% ────────────────▶									
Sit-ups		2 × 20 ────────────────▶									

* Dynamic squats — Athlete drives up onto his toes to complete the squat.
Weights selected for all exercises are light enough to permit explosive movement.

In Phase IV the strength work would be increased to twice per week (days 1 & 4) to allow the strength to be consolidated during mid-season. The athlete should not be too perturbed if there is a slight fall off in the level of weights handled and he should aim to keep within 10% of his winter's peak poundages.

ADVANCED SCHEDULES

Initially the novice lifter will make weekly gains through a combination of strength gains and skill adaptation. The intermediate athlete will naturally not make such rapid advances since skills have been ingrained, but despite this should see monthly increments added to his training diary. The advanced athlete is naturally nearer his ultimate potential and gains in strength become harder and harder to achieve.

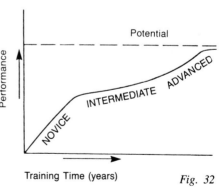

Fig. 32

The programmes outlined thus far for the novice and the intermediate athlete have been straightforward and consistent to enable the athlete to grow in technique and therefore be safe in an environment of fatigue. The early enthusiasm of the novice athlete carries him through the weekly 'grind' of training. The advanced athlete working with such 'regular' schedules will quickly plateau out.

There is a need to introduce variety into the schedule since the body will soon adapt to a regular stimulus. Variety can be introduced on both a weekly and monthly basis.

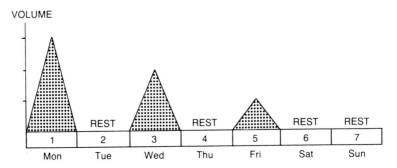

Fig. 33

In the above diagram training has been varied to have three sessions:- one heavy, one medium and one light volume. In terms of hours of hard work this could translate for a thrower of international standard into a three, a two and a one-hour session respectively.

Using a varied volume approach not only stimulates the body into growth by varying the impulse, but also allows the body adequate recovery. The athlete would not be able to sustain three heavy volume sessions each week, but the varied volume approach does allow for at least one maximum volume session.

The theme of variation can also be employed to good effect within a phase and the two examples below show how such variation can be introduced over a three-month period.

Linear variation

Weeks	1 – 3	4 – 7	8 – 10	11 – 12
Repetitions	12	7	5	3
Sets	4	3	4	4
Percentage (intensity)	70%	80%	85%	90%
Total repetitions (volume)	48	21	20	12

Cyclic variation

Weeks	1 – 2	3 – 4	5 – 6	7 – 8	9 – 10	11 – 12
Repetitions	12	7	9	5	7	3
Sets	3	4	3	4	4	5
Percentage (intensity)	70%	80%	75%	90%	80%	95%
Total repetitions (volume)	36	28	27	20	28	15

In the annual cycle it is also important to vary the impulse on a weekly as well as a monthly basis.

Fig. 34 gives some indication of how the volume of strength training will vary during the training year.

Fig. 35 represents the relationship between volume and intensity of training and peak performance — a relationship that the athlete/coach should not forget.

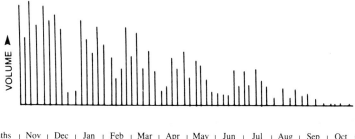

months	Nov	Dec	Jan	Feb	Mar	Apr	May	Jun	Jul	Aug	Sep	Oct
phases	1		2a		2b			3	4		5	6
periods	preparation							competition				trans-ition

Fig. 34

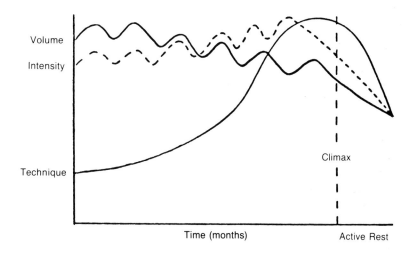

Fig. 35 Periodization for Advanced Athletes

The volume of a strength training unit can be adjusted by the following means:-

(1) Variation of repetitions
(2) Variation of sets
(3) Variation in the number of exercises
(4) Variation in the number of weekly sessions
(5) Variation in the intensity of weight lifted.

The variation of stimulus made on an athlete of advanced standard can be seen as follows using a preparation phase as an example.

35

Microcycle

Phase IIb — 10 weeks (February-April)

Days	1	2	3	4	5	6	7
Work	Strength 'A'		Strength 'B'		Strength 'C'	Strength 'D'	
Day	8	9	10	11	12	13	14
Work	Strength 'A'		Strength 'D'		Strength 'C'	Strength 'D'	

WEEKLY DETAILS AND PROGRESSIONS

Training unit and exercises	Warm ups	Week 1	Week 2	Week 3	Week 4	Week 5	Week 6	Week 7	Week 8	Week 9	Week 10
Strength A (maximum strength)											
Power clean	8-6	4×4 85%	6,5,4,2	4×4 87½%	6,5,4,2	4×4 90%	6,5,4,2	4×4 90%	6,5,4,2	4×4 92½%	6,5,4,2
Bench press	10-8	4×5 85%	8,6,4,2	4×5 87½%	8,6,4,2	4×4 92½%	8,6,4,2	4×3 95%	8,6,4,2	4×2 97½%	8,6,4,2
D/B bench press		3×6		3×6		3×6		3×6		3×6	
Back squat	10-8	3×6 82½%	5×6 82½%	3×6 85%	5×6 85%	3×6 85%	5×6 85%	3×6 87½%	5×6 87½%	3×6 87½%	5×6 90%
Front squat		2×8 70%		2×8 72½%		2×8 72½%		2×8 72½%		2×8 75%	
Push press	10	2×8 70%	8,6,4	2×8 70%	8,6,4	2×8 72%	8,6,4	2×8 75%	8,6,4	2×8 77½%	8,6,4
Varied abdominals		5 min. ——————→			8 min. ——————→			10 min. ——————→			
Strength B											
Fast bench	10	3×5									
Dynamic squats	10	3×5									
Fast D/B press	8	3×5									
Specialist Ex	8	3×6									

WEEKLY DETAILS AND PROGRESSIONS

Training unit and exercises	Warm ups	Week 1	Week 2	Week 3	Week 4	Week 5	Week 6	Week 7	Week 8	Week 9	Week 10
Strength C											
Incline press	10	3×6 85%	3×6 80%	4×6 85%	4×6 80%	4×6 85%	4×6 80%	5×6 85%	5×6 80%	5×6 85%	5×6 80%
Clap press-up	5	5 repetitions sandwiched between each weight set									
Hack squat	10	3×8 75%	4×7 80%	4×8 75%	5×7 80%	5×7 85%	5×7 85%	5×5 85%	5×8 60%	5×5 80%	5×5 85%
Hurdle jumps		5×3′ 0″ hurdles each set									
Power snatch	6	2×6 82½%	4×6 82½%	2×6 82½%	4×6 82½%	2×6 85%	4×6 85%	2×6 85%	4×6 85%	2×6 70%	4×6 87½%
O'head med. ball throw	6	6 throws each set									
Abdominals		3×30									
Strength D (bounds/throws/runs)											
5×4 bounds		↙		↙		↙		↙		↙	
20m×4 stepping			↙		↙		↙		↙		↙
20m×4 hopping		↙		↙		↙		↙		↙	
Standing×10 long jump			↙		↙		↙		↙		↙
Overhead shot×10		6kg ↙		↙		7.26kg ↙		↙		↙	
Forward shot throw			↙		↙		↙		↙		↙
Med. ball push 2×10		↙		↙		↙		↙		↙	
Med. ball thr. o'head 2×10			↙		↙		↙		↙		↙
Harness run (heavy) 4×20			↙		↙		↙		↙		↙
Harness run (light)		↙		↙		↙		↙		↙	

VARIETY IS THE KEY

An athlete's failure to progress is often just simply due to lack of variety — his body has become accustomed to the regular overload placed upon it. There are many and varied ways of overloading — below are just a few such ways:-

Pyramid system

A very popular method of increasing strength. The system involves increasing the weight progressively and at the same time decreases the repetitions as in the example below:-

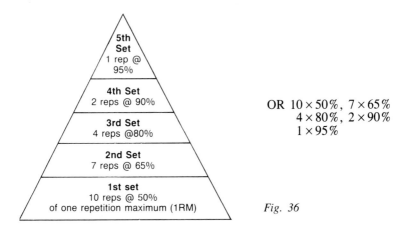

OR 10 × 50%, 7 × 65%
4 × 80%, 2 × 90%
1 × 95%

Fig. 36

The sets and repetitions do not necessarily need to end with a single to be a pyramid system as the following examples show:-
1. 1 × 8, 2 × 5, 3 × 3
2. 1 × 10, 1 × 8, 1 × 5, 1 × 3, 1 × 5, 1 × 8
3. 1 × 10, 2 × 8, 2 × 4, 2 × 2 etc.

The great value of the pyramid system is that it covers all aspects of strength work — high reps for muscle size gains and low reps for strength gains and muscle recruitment.

Forced reps (Burn outs)
The athlete lifts to failure at which point his training partner assists him to complete one or two more repetitions. This is a very effective system for the athlete to break out of a 'plateau' in training but should not be used as a regular part of the schedule.

Negative work
As with the forced reps system, negative work should only be used infrequently.
Here the weight is heavier (120%) than the lifter can overcome and therefore he/she is fighting to arrest the downward path of the weight (Fig. 37). When the weight reaches the bottom position (c) his training partners lift the bar back to the start position (a). This work is very heavy and fatiguing (both physically and mentally) and therefore should be used infrequently. Sets of 3-5 repetitions are suitable for this type of work.

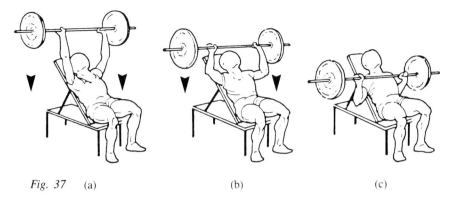

Fig. 37   (a)   (b)   (c)

Supersetting

Two different exercises are combined to produce a superset and the aim is to increase muscle size rather than strength, hence its popularity in body-building. The system is very convenient if time is at a premium. When performing a superset, the athlete completes one lift and then does another with no rest in between. Super-setting can be used in several different ways.

1. Same muscle — the athlete will train the same muscle in both lifts, e.g. bench press followed by dumbell flys.
2. Opposing muscles — working both the agonist and the antagonist sides, e.g. bicep curl followed by tricep extension.
3. Push-pull — one exercise is a pushing motion while the other is a pulling motion, e.g. barbell press followed by bent-over rowing.
4. Upper-lower — one lift works the upper body while the other lift works the lower body, e.g. chins followed by calf raises.

In certain circumstances exercises can be worked in threes (tri-set).

Only perform supersets at the end of a strength session since they are extremely fatiguing.

Pre-exhausted sets

With this system one of the muscle groups involved in a major exercise (e.g. bench press) is pre-exhausted by performing a set (e.g. tricep exercise) in advance so that the weight falls totally upon the non-exercised muscles (e.g. deltoids and pectorals).

Examples

1. Tricep exercise   2. Lateral raise   3. Dumbell flys
   Bench press   Bench press   Bench press

Reducing weight sets

The athlete begins the exercises with a weight that permits five repetitions and no more — at this point the two end discs are taken away to allow two further repetitions, when a further two discs are taken off and two more repetitions completed. This is an excellent method of building muscle mass.

Chapter 4

TECHNIQUE OF LIFTING

THE POWER CLEAN

The lifting of weights is a much neglected skill in athletics, for without such activities the power necessary to move explosively cannot be built. Many injuries inflicted on athletes are attributed to the weights room but are really due to the incorrect lifting of weights — be it free weights, multi-gym, pulleys, etc. Coaches spend many hours on coaching event techniques but only minutes teaching good form in weight-lifting. The power clean is a complex lift requiring both technique and timing, and it is essential that a good basic technique is acquired right at the very onset of lifting.

PC1

PC2

PC3

PC4

Fig. 38 The Power Clean

Starting Position (PC1)

The athlete grasps the bar with a shoulder width grip. The feet are placed hip-width apart with the toes pointing outwards; the bar is positioned over the base of the toes and the body-weight spread evenly over the whole foot for balance. It is important from a safety point of view that the back is kept rigidly flat and the athlete adopts a 90°-100° bend at the knees. The hips should always be higher than the knees. Always ensure that the shoulders are over and slightly in front of the bar. The athlete looks ahead/down at an imaginary focal point two metres in front of the bar.

Floor to Knee (PC2)

Since the shins are angled forwards (PC1) the bar, which rests against them, is to the front of the base and therefore if the bar were to be lifted vertically, the lifter would be forced into a forward weak position. What must happen is that the initial lifting of the bar should be slightly backwards as well as upwards (see Fig. 39) moving the bar into the shins as the bar ascends to the knee. The first stage of the lift is performed by the powerful leg muscles with the back kept flat, maintaining its starting angle and ensuring that the arms are kept straight. Try to think of the arms initially as being a pair of hooks incapable of pulling or bending (PC2).

Fig. 39

It is important to keep the shoulders in front of the bar at this stage and not to try to move the bar by leaning backwards. By the above movements the bar will be lifted to knee height with the bar over the centre line of the foot.

Knee to Chest (PC3)

As the weight passes the knee, the lifter must try to get as close as possible to the bar by forcing the hips up to the bar. This movement will encourage the shoulders to go backwards but the lifter must try to keep his shoulders forward for as long as possible, even at the top of the pull (PC3). Many athletes do not get such full extension but cut the pull short by tugging the shoulders back and jump backwards, thereby losing power. Try to extend all joints of the hips, knee and ankle and keep contact with the floor, for as soon as contact is lost no power can be exerted on the bar.

The Finish (PC4)

The bar is 'received' with a slight bend of the knees high onto the shoulders with the trunk erect. Too many athletes 'catch' the barbell low onto the chest with the trunk leaning back. The elbows must be pushed through and up (PC4) and the barbell load is taken across the shoulders.

Fig. 40
The Power Clean
— Side view

41

THE POWER SNATCH

The power snatch is a superb exercise for developing overall body power with particular emphasis on the leg and lower back muscle. If performed correctly,
the power snatch will assist the athlete in his/her search for power without running the risk of injury they may incur when adopting the deep receiving positions of the competitive snatch.

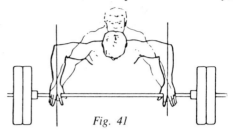

Fig. 41

In the power snatch, the bar is taken from the floor to above the lifter's head in one movement with only a slight knee dip to receive the bar at the top of the lift. The lifter will use a wider grip than the one used to clean or press a barbell. The lifter should take a grip equal to an elbow span when the arms are held out horizontally (Fig. 41).

Starting Positions (PS1)

The feet should be placed at hip width and be slightly turned out. Bodyweight should be evenly distributed over the whole foot. The feet should be positioned under the bar so that the bar is over the joint of the toe and the instep with the shins touching the bar. When the bar is grasped, the back should be flat with a knee angle of about 90°-100°. The shoulders of the lifter should be well over the bar with the head alignment near vertical with the back and with the eye looking ahead.

Floor to Knee (PS2)

As with all athletic events, the strongest muscles are used first and the initial effort must be made with the legs, with the back working statically. Due to the forward inclination of the shins in position PS1, the bar will be a little too far forward to pull vertically, and therefore the initial movement is to ease the bar into the shins, thereby bringing it over the centre of the base of the lifter. The shoulders must be positioned over the bar to stop the tendency of pulling backward. Apart from the initial movement described above, the concept is that of a vertical straight line pull.

Knee to Chest (PS3 & PS4)

The bar at knee height is in a very difficult position, both mechanically and anatomically, and is therefore the potentially weakest part of the whole lift. As the weight passes the knees, the lifter must push his hips up to the bar whilst ensuring that the shoulders are kept over the bar for as long as possible (PS3). The easy option at this point is to pull back rather than driving upwards on to the toes. The lifter at this point should be thinking of a L-O-N-G pull. The arms only unbend at the top of the pull — late and fast (PS4).

The Finish (PS5 & PS6)

At the very top of the pull the lifter must dip under the bar using a slight knee bend, and must keep looking forward keeping his trunk erect. Avoid moving the feet sideways too much since this will result eventually in a grotesque sideways split.

PS1

PS2

PS3

PS4

PS5

PS6

Fig. 42 The Power Snatch

Fig. 43

Never clean or snatch with a bar composed of small discs since the lowness of the bar to the ground will cause an incorrect posture (back parallel to the floor). Always raise the bar by lifting off blocks or use large wooden discs to ensure the correct bar height from the ground.

45

BENCH PRESS

This is by far the most popular lift in the gymnasium and the basic lift for increasing upper body strength.

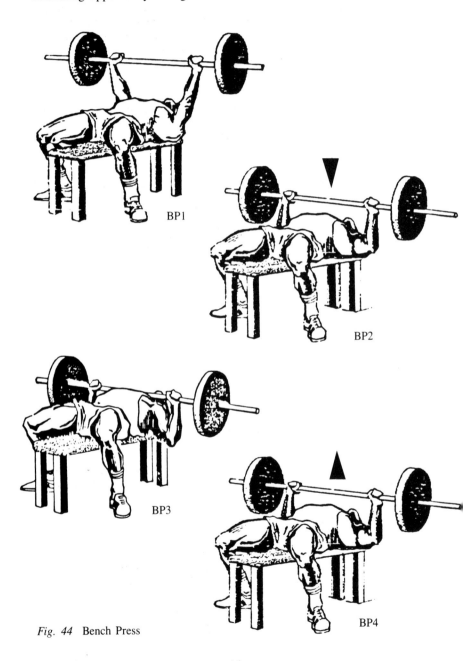

Fig. 44 Bench Press

Starting Position (BP1)

Your starting position should be very stable and balanced. Your feet position should greatly help in keeping you balanced. Note that the feet are flat on the floor and angled slightly outwards which places tension on the thighs, making them rigid and stable. The shoulders and buttocks should touch the bench with the back slightly arched and rigid. The athlete's hand spacing can vary from narrow (placing emphasis on deltoid and triceps) to wide (emphasis on pectoralis) but should be comfortable.

Descent (BP2)

The bar should be lowered down to the chest, not dropped. The lifter should breathe in at the beginning of the descent and, when using a heavy barbell, the breath should be held until the barbell has touched the chest.

The Lift (BP3 & BP4)

The bar should touch/slightly launch off the midchest to low chest area and the lifter should drive the bar slightly backwards, but almost immediately turn the wrists away from the head to ensure that the bar ascends in a vertical path. The athlete should exhale on the latter part of the lift.

Ensure that the bar is pressed up evenly, not favouring one side.

Don't over-arch the back causing the buttocks to leave the bench since this can lead to injury.

UPPER BODY EXERCISE VARIATIONS

Dumbell Flys (DF1 & DF2)

Lying on a bench with the feet raised (DF1) or flat on the floor with the dumbells upright above the chest (DF1). The dumbells are taken down slowly

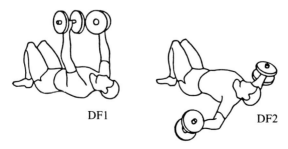

DF1   DF2

sideways breathing in deeply during the descent. The athlete must ensure that the arms gradually become slightly bent to avoid over-straining the elbows and the chest muscle insertion. The dumbells should be taken low enough to stretch the chest muscles (DF2) before returning to the start position, exhaling on the upward movement. An excellent exercise to simulate the discus movement and to ensure range of movement.

Wide Grip Pull-Down (PD1 & PD2)

Taking a wide grip in a fully stretched position (PD1), the athlete should pull the bar down behind the head until it touches the base of the neck (PD2). It is important that the athlete resists on the return to the start position. Breathe in on the way down, out on the way up.

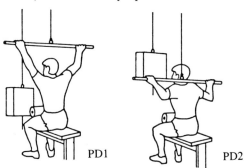

PD1　　　PD2

Wide Grip Chin-up (CU1 & CU2)

A very similar movement to the pull-down exercise, but a much simpler exercise. The movement should be performed slowly, keeping the body straight and throwing the emphasis on the upper back and arm muscles. The sketch shows an overgrasp grip but the exercise can also be performed with an undergrasp grip which throws a greater load on the upper arm (biceps) muscles.

CU1　　　CU2

Bent-over Rowing (BR1 & BR2)

An excellent exercise for upper back strengthening. Using a wide over-grasp grip, the athlete should have his torso parallel to the floor, head up and a

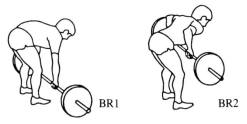

BR1

BR2

hollow lower back (BR1). The knees should be slightly flexed and locked into position. Pull the weight up to the chest. Concentrate on pulling slowly, allowing the upper back muscles to create maximal force. Return the weight to the start position slowly.

Seated Lateral Raise (LR1 & LR2)

The movement should be performed slowly and strictly with the arms very slightly bent until the weight is higher than shoulder level. Slowly lower to the start position. An excellent exercise for developing deltoid muscles.

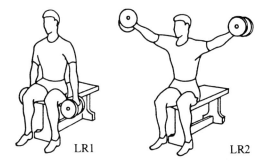

LR1

LR2

Upright Row (UR1 & UR2)

Using a narrow over-grasp grip, the bar should be pulled to the chin keeping the elbows high. Concentrate on developing a rhythmic movement. Excellent in developing shoulders, frontal deltoid and trapezius.

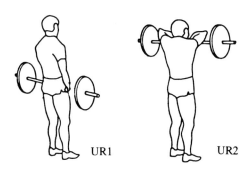

UR1

UR2

Press behind the Neck (PBN1 & PBN2)

Using a shoulder width grip, the bar should be pressed out evenly to arms length using only the shoulder and arm muscles. Return slowly to the start position. The exercise can be performed either seated or standing and is excellent for deltoid development.

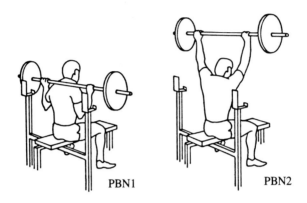

PBN1   PBN2

Incline Press (IP1 & IP2)

Used as a variation of the bench press. The incline press gives greater emphasis to the muscles of the upper chest. From the start position (IP1) the weight should be kept in a straight line both upwards and downwards. The exercise is made even more effective if performed with dumbells with which greater range and control is required.

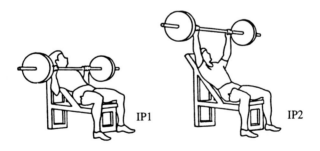

IP1   IP2

ARM EXERCISE VARIATIONS

Parallel Bar Dips (PD1 & PD2)

From a fully extended position (PD1) lower the body into a comfortably low position (PD2). Keeping the elbows out as illustrated and leaning forward will develop the lower chest area, whereas keeping the elbows in and body upright will exercise the tricep muscles of the arm. As strength is acquired, a weight belt or haversack may be worn to provide extra resistance.

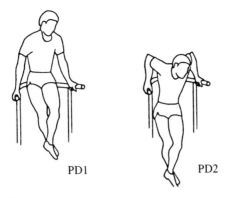

PD1   PD2

Barbell Wrist Curl (WC1 & WC2)

This exercise will develop the forearm muscles and general grip strength. Sitting on the end of a bench, place the back of the lower arms on the thighs, with the hands extended 5 or 6 inches (13-15 cms) from the knee, palms up (WC1). Begin with the barbell in an extended wrist position (WC1) and pull the weight up using only the power of the forearm. The movement should be performed slowly.

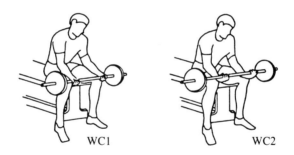

WC1   WC2

Lying Tricep Extension (TE1 & TE2)

Using a narrow grip, the athlete should lie down on a bench with the barbell held overhead (TE1). Lower the bar slowly, keeping the upper arm static until the forehead is touched by the bar. The bar should be pressed back to the start position with a vigorous movement. This is an excellent exercise to develop the tricep muscles of the upper arm.

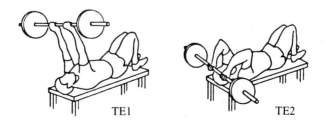

TE1   TE2

Alternate Dumbell Curl (DC1 & DC2)

Holding dumbell weights in a standing position with palms out, alternate each arm with the dumbells passing in mid-point of the range of movement. The curling movement should be even paced; try not to use the body to make it easier to complete. This exercise develops both the biceps and the forearm muscles.

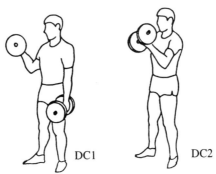

DC1   DC2

TORSO EXERCISES

Back Raise (BE1 & BE2)

With support given to the legs, the athlete lowers the body down to a vertical position (BE2) before slowly returning to the horizontal starting position (BE1). Be careful not to hyper extend since this can cause injury. An excellent lower back exercise.

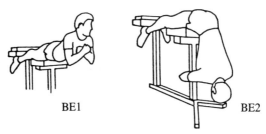

BE1   BE2

Bent Knee Sit-ups (BKS1 & BKS2)

With the feet either supported or unsupported, the athlete lightly clasps his hands behind his neck and adopts the start position (BKS1) with the chin on the chest. Using only the muscles of abdominals, curl the body up to a position where the elbows touch the knees (BKS2). Always perform sit-ups with the knees bent so as to avoid back injuries.

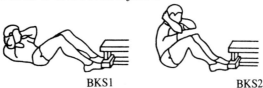

BKS1   BKS2

Sit-up Crunchies (SC1 & SC2)

A variation on the conventional sit-up. Placing the legs on the bench further isolates the abdominals.

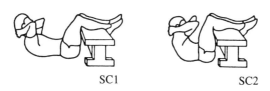

SC1   SC2

Chinnies (C1 & C2)

Lie with the legs extended and the hands lightly clasped behind the head. Simultaneously lift the right elbow and left knee so that they touch (C1) and repeat with the opposite side (C2). An excellent all-round stomach developer.

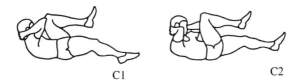

C1   C2

Side Bends (SB1 & SB2)

Hold the dumbell in one hand with the free hand behind the neck (SB1). Slowly lower the dumbell down, keeping the body facing the front. When the oblique muscles are feeling stretched, return vigorously to the start position.

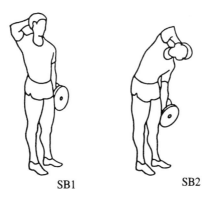

SB1   SB2

THE BACK SQUAT

Starting Position (BS1)

The barbell is taken from a pair of squat stands. This movement must be performed carefully and there must be sensible vigilant spotters standing either side of the bar. The bar is taken on the neck low enough to find the groove which exists at the base of the neck — too high and it will be uncomfortable — too low (powerlifting squat style) and the lift will become too much a back and hip exercise. The bar may be covered with a towel or insulating foam by the novice to make it more comfortable, but eventually such aids will be discarded. The barbell must be firmly grasped to maintain its position throughout the movement. Feet should be comfortably spaced, usually just wider than shoulder width with the toes slightly pointing out. The athlete must be erect, feet tight, and look slightly upwards fixing the gaze on a focal point.

Descending

Fill the lungs via a deep breath and lift the chest high. Keep the head up and back straight when lowering the bar — don't drop down but control the descent which should be slow and sure, keeping the weight off your body and the bar centred directly over the centre of the foot. Letting the weight go over the toes will cause the athlete to round the back. Try to maintain a stiff torso and prevent the back from rounding forward which can easily lead to injury. For those athletes who find it difficult to descend down to a deep position (BS2), raising the heels may be a solution to this problem caused by inflexible ankles or unsuitable leverage.

Upwards Movement

I recommend that the athlete hits a low position where the femur (if exposed) would be seen to be parallel to the ground (BS2). In my experience athletes try to squat higher than this which never really feels comfortable, often unstable and increases the weight to be used. Parallel squatting ensures that a 'groove' is felt and that the athlete feels he is comfortable.

When the lifter hits the parallel position he/she drives upwards ensuring that:-

a) head is forced upwards — drive strongly with the head upwards

b) the back is kept flat and chest high

c) that the hips are forced through

d) knees are turned outwards (BS3).

The latter point is essential since there is a great tendency to let the knees be pulled inwards which forces the hips backwards, this letting the chest come forwards.

Heavy squatting requires that the breath be held from the bottom position to just past the sticking point (BS3), when the air can be expelled. To breathe out at the bottom would cause instability, although when working on high repetitions and low resistance this can be allowed.

It is advisable to wear a leather weight-lifting belt when squatting heavy since this gives support to the stomach and lower back.

BS1   BS2

Fig. 45 The Back Squat

BS3

LEG EXERCISE VARIATIONS

Whilst back squats will form the basis of your leg programme, it is essential that total reliance is not placed upon this exercise. Using a variety of exercises spread over a long period of time will ensure that injuries are avoided.

Leg Extensions (LE1 & LE2)

This exercise isolates the quadricep muscles — make sure that the movement is performed under control without a swinging or bouncing movement. Try holding the top position (LE2) momentarily. A common mistake is to lean back during the upward movement of the weight. Repetitions should range between 5 and 15.

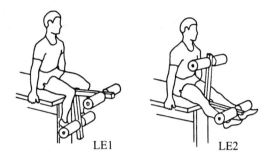

LE1 LE2

Hack Squat (HS1 & HS2)

A very useful piece of apparatus available in the majority of gyms. This exercises the leg muscles without overloading the back. Again, perform the movement with control. The range of movement should be to parallel (HS2).

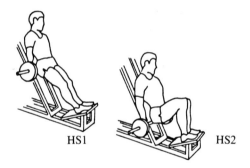

HS1 HS2

Thigh Curls (TC1 & TC2)

An exercise that isolates the hamstrings and buttocks and is very useful to 'balance' the development produced by squatting. It is essential to keep the hips flat down on the bench during the movement. Hold the top position (TC2) for a moment before returning the weight slowly to the start position. Repetitions should be within the range 5-15.

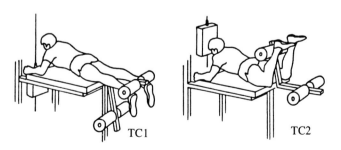

TC1 TC2

Leg Press (LP1 & LP2)

A leg isolation exercise — perform the exercise slowly ensuring that the weight is returned to the start position with resistance and not with a 'freefall'. Care must be taken with those machines which place the athlete with his back horizontal since there is a tendency to cheat by raising the buttocks which can lead to injury.

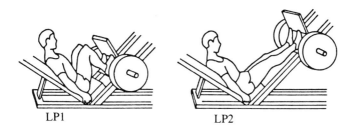

LP1   LP2

Toe Raise (TR1 & TR2)

This replaces the more conventional calf raise with the barbell held across the shoulders, which can be extremely heavy and uncomfortable. The apparatus can be replaced by simply putting a barbell across the knees.

All of the above exercises are isolation exercises and therefore do not develop, as do back squats, the co-ordinated leg strength needed for athletics. Therefore use these exercises to supplement barbell squats, not as a replacement.

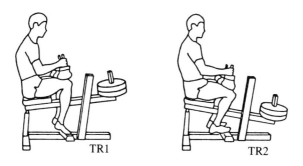

TR1   TR2

BARBELL ALTERNATIVES

Front Squat (FS1 or FS2)

The front squat places greater emphasis on the thigh muscles and less on the lower leg/buttocks than does the conventional back squat. The bar is held across the shoulders, either cross-armed (FS1) or in a clean grip with the elbows held high. The movement is similar to that of the back squat, but it is essential to maintain an upright position or the bar will be lost forwards.

Splits Squats (SS1 & SS2)

Exercises the upper leg and hip extensions and is suitable for the sprinter, jumper and javelin thrower. Ensure that the bar is stable on the shoulders and perform with rhythm, alternating the legs. Repetitions above 5 are suitable.

	Sprints and Hurdles	Endurance	Horizontal Jumps	Pole Vault	High Jump	Shot	Discus	Hammer
Pulling Exercises								
Power Clean	X	X	X	X	X	X	X	X
Power Snatch	X	—	X	X	X	X	X	X
Dead Lift	—	—	—	—	—	/	/	X
Heavy Pulls	—	—	—	—	—	/	/	/
Leg Exercises								
Back Squat	X	X	X	X	X	X	X	X
Front Squat	/	/	/	/	—	/	/	X
Hack Squat	/	—	—	/	—	—	—	—
Leg Press	/	—	/	—	—	—	—	—
Toe Raise	X	X	X	/	X	—	—	—
Thigh Curls	X	—	/	/	/	/	/	/
Thigh Extensions	/	—	—	—	/	—	—	—
Split Squat	/	X	X	/	/	—	—	—
Upper Body Exercises								
Bench Press	X	/	/	/	/	X	X	—
Incline Press	—	—	—	—	—	X	—	—
Press B/neck	/	—	/	/	/	/	/	/
Lateral Raise	—	—	—	/	—	/	/	/
Upright Row	—	—	—	/	—	—	—	—
Bent-over Rowing	—	—	—	—	—	/	/	X
Pull-downs	—	—	/	/	—	—	—	/
Chins	/	—	—	X	—	—	—	/
Flys	—	—	—	—	—	/	X	—
Arm Exercises								
Dips	/	—	—	X	—	/	/	—
Wrist Curls	—	—	—	—	—	—	—	—
Tricep Extensions	—	—	—	/	—	X	—	—
Dumbell Curls	X	/	/	/	/	—	/	—
Torso Exercises								
Back Hypers	—	/	/	/	/	/	/	X
Side Bends	—	—	—	—	—	X	X	/
Bent Knee Sit-ups	/	/	X	X	X	X	X	X
Crunchies	/	/	/	/	/	/	/	/
Chinnies	X	/	X	X	X	X	X	X

X = Essential   / = Good Assistance Exercise   — = Non-essential

Chapter 5

FREE-WEIGHT STRENGTH DEVELOPMENT

NON-BARBELL METHODS OF STRENGTH TRAINING

Much of this book has dealt with barbell training since this is by far the most common and arguably the most effective means of increasing basic strength. The athlete/coach must look upon the barbell as being only the part solution to his strength training needs for there are very many other vehicles for improving strength, especially event specific strength.

Circuit Training

During the 1950's circuit training was firmly established as the prime fitness exercise regime for all sports and the book 'Circuit Training' by R.E. Morgan and G.T. Adamson (1957 — price 10s 6d), sat upon the shelves of all physical education establishments, well thumbed and carrying no dust for lack of use. Geoff Dyson, the then Chief National Coach, wrote in the foreword to this book: "In their efforts towards the proper physical preparation of the athlete, the national coaches have turned to circuit training. They like its adaptability to the needs of the individual; its simplicity. Above all, they know the value of having the athletes themselves observe and assess their improvement in fitness, as the authors claim. Such training is no mere adjunct to preparation for a specific event; it is fundamental to it."

Since the fifties, the popularity of circuit training has waxed and waned, but today it has re-emerged as an indispensable part of conditioning the modern athlete. Circuit training is a widely used and proven method of improving muscular endurance, general fitness, muscular strength and power — depending upon the design and type of circuit used.

Circuits are many and varied, but usually consist of a series of exercises performed one after another until the circuit of exercises is completed. When designing the circuit, the coach must have in mind the following:-

1. The circuit must be tailored to suit individual needs and rates of improvement.

2. Exercises performed must be strenuous.

3. Exercises selected must be simple to perform, since skill always breaks down under fatigue.

4. Exercises must be readily standardised. It is essential for the performer to know how much work he is doing.

5. There should be no attempt to separate training for strength from training for muscular endurance. It is likely that all exercises of less than 25 repetitions will have an effect on both elements — exercise at the lower end will emphasize strength and those exercises at the upper end will emphasize muscular endurance.

6. In practice, circuit training increases muscular endurance rather than strength. Therefore it may be advisable to include some exercises with less than 10 repetitions maximum in the circuit.

7. All areas of the body should be included in a circuit although bias can be directed towards the athlete's event.

8. Exercises in the circuit should be arranged so that body parts are alternated, and likewise exercises that cause great stress should be alternated with less stressful ones.

   Below are three types of circuit:-

(a) General fitness circuits

(b) Elastic strength circuit

(c) Body-part conditioning circuits.

   GENERAL CIRCUITS — the choice is limitless, but the following are two of the most popular:-

Set Time Circuits

Choose about eight to ten exercises, e.g. press-ups, sit-ups, vertical jumps, knee raises, step-ups, rope climb, hurdle jumps, hyper-extensions. Each member of the squad performs as many of the repetitions as is possible in 20 seconds, followed by 30 seconds rest which includes moving to the next exercise. After completing all exercises (a set), five minutes rest is given

Press-ups   Sit-ups   Knee Raises   Rope Climb   Hyper-extension   Step-ups   Vertical jumps   Hurdle Jumps

Fig. 46

before commencing the next set of exercises. The advantages of this version of circuit training are:-

i) Athletes of differing abilities can train together, e.g. the experienced athlete completes 20 press-ups in 20 seconds, the beginner only 8, yet both are working to maximum.

ii) Large numbers are easily handled — you only need a watch and a whistle.

iii) Progression is easy — more exercise, more repetitions, more exercise time, less recovery, more sets, less recovery between sets or a combination of all — permutations are endless.

Conditioning Circuit

Development	No. of exercises	Exercise duration	Recovery	Sets	Rest between sets
Novice	8	20 secs.	30 secs.	2	5 mins.
Intermediate	8	30 secs.	30 secs.	3	5 mins.
Advanced	11	30 secs.	20 secs.	2	10 mins.

Set Number Circuits

The athlete will test himself to find out his maximum number of repetitions of a particular exercise, either in a set time, e.g. 60 seconds, or to failure depending upon the nature of the exercise. The exercises are then put together in a circuit and the prescribed number of repetitions, rests and sets are completed.

Dosage	Exercise	Repetitions	
If included normally done 2-6 times per week over 2-4 weeks introduction block. Sometimes done instead of stage in basic block.	Press-ups	50% max.	Progression:— is by number of circuits per session. Increased by 1 every week, commencing with 3 circuits. Two minutes recovery between circuits. Maximum number of circuits 6. Retest for maximum if continued beyond 4 weeks. Also consider competing against the clock after 4 weeks
	Burpees	50% max. in 45 secs.	
	Curls (abd.)	50% max. in 60 secs.	
	Broken Cradles	50% max. in 60 secs.	
	Pull-ups	50% max.	
	Speedball	8 × 60 secs.	

Recovery: 2 mins. between circuits.
No rest between exercises.

Fig. 47 (from Dick 1987)

The general fitness circuit has its place in the schedule throughout the whole of the winter, but especially at the start of the winter campaign when the athlete is 'training to train' — there is no better method of getting fit quickly.

ELASTIC STRENGTH CIRCUIT

The exercises chosen are those that require a fast, repetitive, explosive execution, e.g. clap press-ups, depth jumps, medicine ball throw, hopping and bounding. Since the aim is to increase the athlete's elastic strength, the work time is short (say 10 seconds) and the rest time enough to ensure good recovery for the next exercise (say 30 seconds). Although not the objective of such circuits, specific endurance is improved.

Such circuits would be performed during the second half of the winter period, building upon the fitness base established by the general circuits, and are not progressed beyond the end of the preparation phase of the winter schedule.

BODY-PART CONDITIONING CIRCUITS

These are used to prevent injury of a stressed area, e.g. knees, lower back. Often athletes train very specifically, such as performing many hundreds of squats with heavy weights, which do strengthen the legs massively (i.e. quadriceps) but leave some supporting muscles relatively weak. Often great force is exerted upon the joints by strengthened muscle and injury occurs because of imbalance. To counteract this problem, circuits are performed concentrating on one joint area such as the following:-

CIRCUIT 1
1. free standing squats × 20 (to bench)
2. squat thrusts × 50
3. side sitting (kneeling to sides) × 20 (must keep both knees on the floor).
4. kneel to stand to kneel × 30 — see fig. 1.

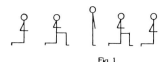

Fig. 1.

5. step ups × 80
6. jumping with feet astride bench to squat × 40 —see fig 2.

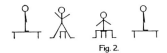

Fig. 2.

7. cross leg squats × 20
8. hop on weakest leg 1 min
9. crab walking

CIRCUIT 2
1. stand from bench × 20
2. step ups × 50
3. running on the spot × 1 min
4. free standing squats × 1 min
5. lying on back, hips and knees bent, hip raise strong leg out in front — hold × 1 min. (fig. 3.)

Fig. 3.

6. press ups × 20
7. press up quadriceps strengthener — see fig. 4.

Fig. 4.

8. squat against wall × 2 min
9. sit ups × 30

Fig. 48

63

CIRCUIT 3
1. running around gym
2. squat on low rung × 10, one foot
3. maximum free standing squats in 2 mins
4. medicine ball strengthener — see fig. 5.

Fig. 6.

Fig. 5.

5. press ups × 30
6. crab walking
7. free standing squats without hands × 20
8. one leg squats
9. leaning against wall, one leg out in front at a time × 20 each leg — see fig. 6.

CIRCUIT 4
1. sit ups × 30
2. squat against wall sliding up and down wall × 30
3. sprint starts × 30
4. bunny jumps
5. bench squats × 50
6. crossleg squats × 20
7. cycle 1 mile
8. press ups × 20

Fig. 48 continued

The above circuits were prescribed by the Physiotherapy Department of Southampton General Hospital (February 1982) for a GB international shot putter recovering from a knee operation.

Such circuits are valuable to the healthy athlete during the early winter period but, since the principle of reversibility applies to all, it is a good idea to keep them going throughout the year.

BOUNDING AND HOPPING

Undoubtedly bounding and hopping are two activities which greatly increase the elastic strength of the legs. It should be pointed out that only the mature athlete with a background of conditioning can undertake such practices to a significant degree; youngsters should perform jumping 'a little and not too often'.

Before a hopping session the coach/athlete should ensure:-

(a) that the jumping surface is compatible for such activities — that it is flat with some 'give', e.g. a good grass surface, thin gymnastic mats or the softer type of synthetic running surfaces.

(b) the athletes wear good quality footwear that has a cushioned sole but not too thick so as to make the ankle unstable.

As with any strengthening exercise, the technique must be correct as this will ensure that all the benefits are derived from the activity and that the risk of injury is kept to a minimum.

Technique

1. The athlete should aim to strike the ground with a flat foot contact — this does not actually happen since the heel will strike a fraction ahead of the toe. The concept of a 'flat foot' is a good one for the athlete to think about.

2. In single foot bounding/jumping, the foot performs a reaching and pawing action (Fig. 49) as the foot approaches and goes through its landing actions. N.B. Never, ever 'stab' the leg at the ground during landings, as this will lead to a jarred back and bruised heels.

3. Keep the torso erect, flat and stable when bounding and avoiding 'piking' which is caused by letting the backside stick out.

4. For the non-specialist jumper, the arm action should be alternating, balancing the work of the legs.

Active pawing
action

Flat foot
landing
under body

Torso erect, eyes
looking forward.
Vigorous
take-off.

Fig. 49

The athlete must be competent at the basic movement before extensive work is undertaken. An introductory session using only six foot contacts could be as follows:-

(i) Hop right foot (ii) hop left foot (iii) stepping
(iv) hop-hop — step-step rhythm.

This could be regarded as one set and the number of sets could be increased with improved conditioning, as could the number of foot contacts up to a maximum of 12.

Two-footed contact jumps

A variation of hopping and bounding, but with the important technique difference that the athlete will make foot contact toe first.

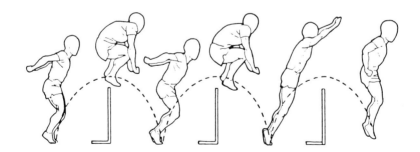

Fig. 50 Jumping exercises using hurdles

Since these exercises are of a slower and therefore more strength related nature, the athlete should build up to a maximum of six foot contacts, although lower numbers do not necessarily mean less gains.

With both hopping/bounding and two-footed contact jumps, as the season approaches the emphasis should be on lighter, faster foot contacts and on speed rather than height/length of jump.

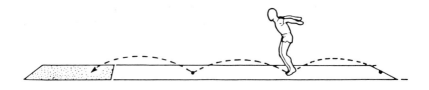

Fig. 51 Jumping exercises using a sand pit

PLYOMETRICS

It is well documented that if a muscle is pre-stretch or made to build up high tension it will concentrically contract with much greater force. Plyometrics make use of this factor by, for instance, an athlete dropping down from a low box and immediately driving upwards (stretch reflex). In this example the contraction of the thigh muscle is exceptional and does develop elastic leg strength. The key factor of such 'stretch reflex' work is that the response upon ground contact must be immediate; not to do so would make the exercise a concentric contraction and not involve the stretch reflex. Dropping down from a box which is too high would create a loading which is too great and therefore the athlete would not be able to respond quickly. Depth jumping heights will depend upon the strength of the athlete concerned, but heights of up to 40 cms should be adequate since this can generate tensions of up to seven times bodyweight.

Plyometric exercises are extremely stressful and their inclusion in the athlete's programme must be well thought out. The younger athlete must be introduced to plyometrics only after an initial period of overall conditioning to ensure that sufficient leg strength has been acquired. Verhoshansky (Soviet Union) estimates

Fig. 52

that his research has indicated that an athlete should be able to back squat twice his own bodyweight before being strong enough to do plyometrics. This may be an extreme measure but indicates that the athlete must be strong to benefit.

No such training should be utilised before the onset of puberty. Athletes post-puberty must complete long and well conceived conditioning programmes before they get involved in plyometric exercises. Jumping over ropes and skipping, similar to young children in every day activity, are good conditioners to prepare for plyometrics. For the beginner one session is sufficient. The advanced athlete can handle up to three sessions per week at selected times of the year — rest must be 48 hours.

Medicine Ball Work

The medicine ball is an excellent piece of equipment for developing elastic strength and for conditioning the whole body. Medicine balls are unsuitable for developing general strength since the weight of the ball would have to be such that it could easily lead to injury of the limbs of the body.

Repetitions will vary from six to thirty depending upon what fitness element the athlete is aiming to improve. Medicine balls vary and are usually commercially on sale between 2kg to 7kg, although heavier implements can be improvised.

Training unit and exercises		Week 1	Week 2	Week 3		Week 4	Week 5	Week 6
Two-hand push	4kg	2×10	3×10	3×10	5kg	2×10	2×10	3×10
Overhead throw	3kg	2×10	2×10	3×10	4kg	2×10	2×10	3×10
Overhead (backward)	4kg	—	2×10	—	5kg	—	2×10	—
Sit-up & throw	3kg	1×10	2×10	2×10	4kg	1×10	2×10	2×10
Hammer delivery	4kg	1×10	—	1×10	5kg	1×10	—	2×10

Fig. 53 Medicine Ball schedule

Fig. 54 Medicine Ball Exercises

MULTIGYM MACHINES (FIXED PATH WEIGHTS)

'Multigym' is the brand name of an apparatus that has assembled on a large frame exercise stations that make use of fixed path movements using pulleys and weight stacks. In recent years there has been a mushrooming of such equipment so that they appear in almost every town, either in the local sports centre, school or fitness centre. In many ways they have revolutionised strength-training making it accessible to all ages and social classes. The advantages of such equipment are:-

1. It requires very little skill to use the equipment since the weights move in a pre-determined path.
2. Since load increases/decreases can be made within seconds, many people can use a 'multigym' at one session.
3. It is extremely safe to train on since it is almost impossible to drop a weight stack upon oneself.

It is an ideal piece of apparatus for the novice to commence strength-training with, since it requires little skill learning. For the young athlete it appears to be perfectly safe since the majority of its exercise stations are not load bearing and therefore the potential risk of an injury to the spine is minimal.

The drawback to most machines is that they provide single joint exercises. Since the athlete moves in multi-joint movements, these exercises are perhaps not quite as advantageous as the training performed with barbells. Machines also do not work the stabilizing muscles as much because the weight is sup-

Core exercises — basic exercises plus alternatives

	Basic exercise		Variations	
1. Chest	Bench press	Peck-deck	Pullovers	Incline press
2. Back	Lat pull down	Seated rowing	Pullovers	Bent over row
3. Front thighs	Seated leg press	Leg extensions	Hack squats	Squats
4. Rear thighs	Leg curls	Seated leg press	Hip & back extensor	
5. Shoulders	Upright rows	Shoulder press	Lateral raise	Shoulder shrugs
6. Abdomen/low back	Sit-ups	Knee raises Hip flexor	Side bends	Trunk twisting
7. Lower legs	Calf raise	Toe press (leg press)		
8. Upper arm – front	Bicep curls	Preacher curl	Undergrasp chins	Narrow grip pull-downs
9. Upper arm – rear	Tricep push down – Lat	Tricep press powercam	Dips	French press
10. Forearms	Wrist roller	Wrist curls	Wrist gripper	
11. Neck optional	Shoulder shrugs	Neck machine		

From 'Multigym Basic Instructor Manual', Powersport

68

ported. The athlete does not have to control the weight, so the stability of the joint is not as good as it could be using free weights. Since machines work on isolated muscle groups, it is not possible to do exercises where many muscle groups are involved so that all that area is of proportioned strength.

Machines do have their good points since some muscles are better trained by machines and you can, of course, isolate a particular area. This is excellent for working weak areas or working around an injury.

Multigym Schedules

The basic principles that have been prescribed for the barbell are exactly the same for fixed apparatus — principles of strength never change.

Powersport International Limited have produced a list of core exercises for use with their multigym equipment (see opposite).

Fixed path apparatus is also ideal for a training group to perform circuit training upon. The circuit below can be performed on a basic multigym apparatus:-

A. A TYPICAL PROGRAMME USING A 13-STATION MULTIGYM
   (clockwise)

 1. Shoulder press
 2. Leg extensions/leg curls
 3. Bench press
 4. Abdominal sit-ups
 5. Jump dips
 6. Seated leg press
 7. Lat. pull-downs
 8. Back hyperextensions
 9. Seated rowing/bicep curls
10. Hip flexion

1. 12-15 repetitions with 70% load of 5 RM.
2. Recovery between exercises 20 secs.
3. 2-3 circuits.

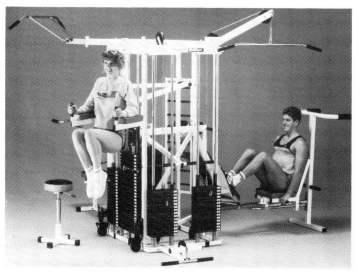

Multigym type of equipment is an ideal piece of apparatus for the novice to commence strength training

Chapter 6

THE YOUNG ATHLETE

Sport has an increasing influence on our daily lives and its importance to children and parents has increased dramatically. Competitive sport now reaches the very young. Leagues and championships are no longer confined to the late teens. The motivation of winning has brought organised training to the very young, and the previously taboo area of strength training is now likely to be taken on board by the enthusiastic coach or parent in order to ensure success. Is this desirable? Are there dangers? Do many young athletes simply get a modified adult programme?

Strength-training, whether it is for adults, children or women, follows the same well-tried principles:-

1. *Overload* — the muscle must be forced to work hard for the cross-sectional area to increase, and with it increase strength. Performing light weights easily will not produce strength gains.

2. *Reversibility* — the muscle must be regularly stimulated to ensure strength gains and by the same token, if left unstimulated, strength will be lost.

3. *Specificity* — exercise must be specific to the type of strength required and therefore is related to the demands of the event.

Can these principles be applied to a very young athlete? A look must be taken at the young physique.

'Lifting heavy weights will stunt your growth'

There is no evidence that this 'old wives tale' is true, e.g. a Soviet study (Yurachenkov) comparing swimmers with weightlifters in the 14-17 age range found that the growth patterns were the same in both sports. It is true that weightlifters tend to be shorter, but this is a natural selection process since shorter levers are mechanically more efficient at lifting heavy weights. Tall, thin boys will quickly leave the sport through lack of success.

'Weightlifting will cause joint injury'

The bones of the young are more elastic, yet have less bending strength than in the adult skeleton. The effect on bone growth of moderate training is clearly positive, but *excessively* biased loading may have a damaging effect. It is questionable whether weight-training would affect this area since the amount of time spent actually *lifting* weights is calculated at only 0.0011% of a week. Since growth plate damage *may* be caused by overuse, the more rigorous and continuous pastimes of team games may be potentially more dangerous and it still remains to be seen if this sensitive area of children's anatomy remains immune to the increasingly rigorous training the young are subjected to.

Potentially the spine and related areas are more at risk through heavy lifting since the support given to this complicated structure by the torso muscles is somewhat lacking in the young. Torso strength develops late in the growth cycle, and loads carried above the head or on the shoulders may lead to injury if the technique is not correctly performed.

'Strength is for men, not boys'

There is a school of thought that advocates that strength training should not take place until after puberty, due to the fact that there is a lack of muscle building hormones (e.g. testosterone) present in the young body. Research evidence is not conclusive although recent studies (Micheli 1983, Sewall & Micheli 1984) have indicated that significant strength gains can be made in pre-pubescent males and females. As previously explained, strength can be increased either through increasing the cross sectional area of the muscle or by better recruitment of muscle fibres via the central nervous system. It is most probably through the latter avenue that strength is increased in the pre-pubescent child.

A 15-year-old has 27% muscle mass as compared to the 44% of a 19-year-old and therefore loadings should be adjusted to take into account the lack of muscle in the young physique.

'Strength training is unsuitable for girls'

Girls develop faster and stop growing earlier (Fig. 55). They are approximately two years in advance of boys in development and therefore can be introduced to formalised strength training earlier. Women have narrower shoulders and broader hips than men. Different angles of tendon attachment to, and of muscle alignment with, bone reduces the efficiency of muscle pull and increases injury potential.

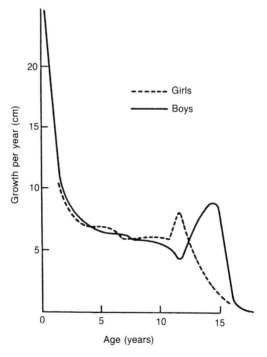

Fig. 55 Mean growth rates (in cm per year)(Bayley, from *Prader*)

71

Strength training can be introduced in an organised way as soon as the girl finishes her adolescent growth spurt. Strength training should be progressed more gently than for men. Since girls have a weaker support system and less skeletal muscle mass than boys, the loading given should reflect this deficiency.

Basic Rules

Strength development of young athletes should be based on the established principles of basic training, aiming for a many-sided technical and physical development.

● Specific strength improvement to force the performance level of a particular event is not recommended.

● The development of strength must fit into the framework of an all-round training procedure and is not to be singled out for preferential attention.

● Considerable attention in training should be directed at development of those muscles which stabilize the spine on the pelvis (abdominals and lower back) and the rotation of the spine.

● Until the growing has stabilised in bone-joint development, it is inadvisable to load the spine when exercising. Unless the athlete has an extensive background of general strength work which has systematically developed the musculature supporting the spine, heavy weights should not be taken on the shoulders or held above the head.

● It is essential that all strength exercises are performed correctly and it is therefore essential that competent coaching is given during the early skill learning phase.

● The number of exercises attempted should be restricted to ensure that good technique is acquired. In acquiring good technique it is necessary to embark upon a learning period where the load is light and the repetitions numerous.

● Initially the strength units should be short in duration with adequate recovery between exercises allowed. This will permit good exercise technique.

● Encourage the routine of warming-up for strength work — injuries occur through either lack of warm-up or incorrect technique or a combination of both.

● Extreme passive mobility or endurance work should not follow an extensive strength work-out since this will increase the possibility of connective tissue injury.

Certain exercises should be avoided when involving the young, growing physique:-

Heavy conventional sit-ups or leg raises.

Deep knee-bending.

Good morning exercises.

Jarring work, especially on hard surfaces.

DEVELOPING A PROGRAMME

Before commencing regular strength training, an important factor to be taken into consideration is the mental maturity of the athlete, i.e. is he/she mature enough to follow advice and directions. Work with machines, weight stacks and especially loose weights must require a serious adult approach.

When considering designing a programme for an athlete, the coach must consider the type of strength required (elastic, absolute, endurance) and the type of muscle activity (concentric, isometric, eccentric). Before such factors are taken into account, the athlete must go through a period of general strengthening work that will build a base upon which specialised strength work can safely be attempted.

It is a mistake to assume that the only avenue for strength development is the barbell and dumbell. The principles of 'overload' can operate in a variety of activities.

Strengthening activities

Weights — the most generally used form of strength work, but heavy weights are generally unsuitable for the sub-16 age group where barbell and dumbell work should be limited to *light* technique work.

Multi-gym — or similar apparatus. An excellent lead-in to weight-training with little or no danger of injury and little technique needed. The majority of the stations (exercises) do not involve loading the spine and therefore leg work can be attempted.

Running — sprint starts, uphill sprints, harness-work — all develop explosive, elastic strength.

Jumping — a large variety of jumps can be attempted and measured (motivation), but remember that the landing area should have 'give', e.g. gym mats, grass. Correct technique should be taught.

Depth jumping (Plyometrics) — should be avoided by the very young age groups since it places a great load upon the knees. When introduced, it should be gradual with heights not exceeding 80 cms and the landing area having 'give' (gym mats).

Bodyweight exercises — old stand-bys such as the press-up and the sit-up are excellent for forming a basis of strength. By increasing/decreasing the leverage, exercises can be progressive. Gymnastic apparatus exercises are very effective strength builders.

Circuit training — an excellent activity for increasing both fitness and strength. An essential part of the development of the young athlete, it enables the coach to direct a session for a large group with little or no apparatus.

Isometrics — not too relevant to the dynamic sport of athletics. Strengthening in a specific static position may be useful for the mature athlete, e.g. the torso position in the long jump take-off.

Throwing — using shots and medicine balls etc. can provide an enjoyable method of developing explosive strength in the rotational direction.

PHASE ONE

Pre-puberty (under 11 girls, under 12 boys)

The 9-11 age group can be approached in the same manner for boys and girls, although boys will move to more advanced work a little later than girls.

AIM — all-round strength development in a fun environment.

EXERCISES — mainly partner and bodyweight exercises:- pushing/pulling, hopping, climbing, games with light medicine balls, exercises on gymnastic forms, boxes and simple apparatus (Fig. 56). The choice of exercise should be varied to avoid boredom, but limited to the extent that exercises must be well-performed.

FREQUENCY — one strength unit per week (twice per week for advanced youngsters).

PROGRESSION — Calisthenics can be introduced later with single set many repetitions practised. Again exercise should be correctly performed.

Fig. 56

PHASE TWO
12-14 girls, 13-15 boys
Children are moving into a period of growth spurt and it is essential that all-

round development is stressed. Emphasis should be placed upon torso development in order that stability is ensured for more advanced/specialised work to follow.

AIM — all round strength — torso development — good technical model.

METHOD — Sessions previously practised can be continued, but strength circuits can be introduced (Fig. 57).

CIRCUITS — In a club/school environment the best method of developing strength in the young athlete is via circuit training. Bodyweight only should be used and the exercises practised and established before putting them into the circuit.

The variations of circuit are many and varied and the circuits below are examples taken from Training Theory by F.W. Dick (Fig. 57) and by Dr. Hans-Peter Liffler (G.D.R.) (Fig. 58).

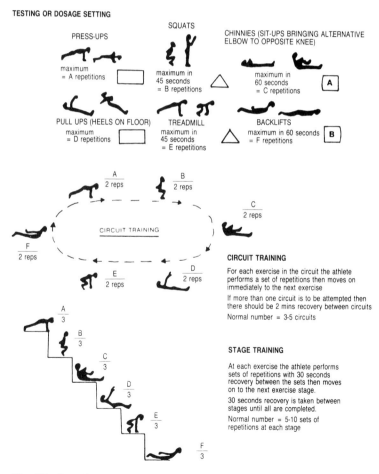

Fig. 57 Organisation of circuit and stage training

75

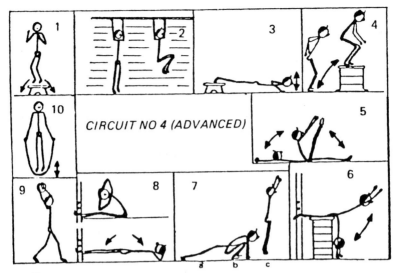

Fig. 58

1. Double-leg take-off jumps on and off bench (20 to 40cm) (legs and feet).
2. Knee lifts on a wall ladder (abdominal).
3. Push-ups with feet elevated on a bench (arm extension).
4. Jumping on and off a gymnastic box (60cm) (leg extensors).
5. Sit-ups into V-position (abdominal).
6. Trunk and arm lifts on a box with feet supported (back).
7. Front support jumps into crouch position and then upwards (complex).
8. Twisting sit-ups with feet supported (abdominal).
9. Double-arm and overhead medicine ball throws against the wall from 2.50m (8′ 2½″) distance (shoulders, arms, chest).
10. Double-legged skipping (legs and feet).

Number of Exercises	Exercise Time (sec.)	Recoveries between exercise (sec.) rounds (min.)		Total time for		
				2 rounds	3 rounds	4 rounds
3	15	30 (sec.)	3 (min.)	6.30	11.15	16.00
4	15	30	3	8.00	13.30	19.00
5	15	30	3	9.30	15.45	22.00
6	15	30	3	11.00	18.00	25.00
7	15	30	3	12.30	20.15	28.00
8	15	30	3	14.00	22.30	31.00
9	15	30	3	15.30	24.45	34.00
10	15	30	3	17.00	27.00	37.00

PHASE THREE
15-16 girls, 16-17 boys

In this post-puberty period more specialised work can commence, although the all-round development is still the key element.

Endurance Events

1st year

Circuits, but with resistance being used. Multi-gyms are excellent for such work since they are safe and exercises easily learned. No attempt should be made to divert away from general exercises.

2nd year

Progression on to timed circuits to develop strength endurance.

3rd year

(i) Circuits continued — barbells used if weakness is a limiting factor for an athlete.

Explosive Events

1st year

(i) Using multi-gym, the athlete would use a simple set method (3 sets of 10) using basic exercises.
(ii) Barbells and dumbells used with light weights, high repetitions — technique emphasized.
(iii) Multiple jumps, bounding.

2nd year

Progression onto conventional weights, but restricted to exercises that *don't* load the spine (see below). Depth jumping introduced.

3rd year

Conventional weights used — spine load-bearing exercises are restricted to high rep-fast movements which limit the amount of weight being used, e.g. 10 repetitions in 20 seconds.

EXAMPLE
PHASE THREE — Year Two (explosive events)

Weight programme			*Effect*
Power clean		$8-6-6-6$	(complex — legs/back)
Bench press		$10-8-6-6$	(chest/shoulders)
Dumbell jump squat		$10-10-10$	(legs)
Super set	Lateral raise	$10-10$	(shoulders)
	Curls	$8-8$	
Super set	D/b calf raise	$15-15$	
	Hyper raises	$10-10$	
	Partial sit-ups	$15-15-15$	
	Leg raises	$15-15-15$	

Duration — 50 mins./60 mins.

From the progressions shown an athlete can specialise from this base of firm, all-round conditioning.

Chapter 7

STRENGTH TRAINING FOR WOMEN

Until recent years, strength training for women has proved a difficult area to organise, motivate and programme. The 1980's witnessed almost a revolution in western society through the popularity of fitness regimes for women. Women who had previously been excluded from fitness gymnasiums became 'big business' and took to lifting weights in the pursuit of improved physical shape and fitness. This in turn has made the introduction of strength work much easier for the trackside coach, since females practising such work is no longer considered 'freaky' in society.Women athletes now approach strength training in a much more positive way which will lead to much higher strength gains.

"I am convinced that no female athlete will develop strength by means of discipline-specific training against her will, but will do so as a result of her own decision" — Ruth Fuchs (G.D.R.), IAAF Congress 9-11 December 1983.

Many coaches view women as being the weaker sex and downgrade strength work accordingly. Pound for pound, women are as strong as men. It is generally agreed that, in absolute terms, women possess approximately two-thirds of the strength of a man. When bodyweight and size are taken into

'Pound for pound, women are as strong as men.'

account, women are much closer to men in strength and indeed some studies (Wilmore, 1974, Hoffman, Stauffer & Jackson, 1979) have indicated that relative to lean body mass, women's leg strength is equal to that of men. Wilmore goes further and claims that women are actually 5.8% stronger than the male when strength is expressed relative to lean body mass.

Women tend to be initially relatively weak in their upper bodies but exhibit good leg strength. Wilmore (1974) reported that when body mass is taken into account, women are weaker than men in the upper body. There appears to be a variation from muscle to muscle — the hip extensors and flexors are the strongest groups in females with the chest, shoulders and arms being the most weak, possibly due to the socialisation choice of activities (Fox and Matthews, 1981).

It is a commonly held belief that women benefit less from strength work than do men. This is totally untrue and female strength work is just as beneficial for women as it is for men. Women can become extremely strong and lifts of 300kg back squat and approaching 200kg in the bench press have been witnessed.

When undergoing strength work, women increase their strength at the same or even greater rate than do men (Wilmore 1974, 1978). The reason put forward for the superior strength gains in women is that they have probably started from a lower base level than do men and therefore are not as close to their genetic potential as are men. It is interesting to note that Wells' (1985) research points towards women reaching their strength peak at around 30 years of age, which is later than for men, and maintaining it longer.

A fear expressed by the majority of women athletes is that strength training will lead to excessive hypertrophy and therefore they will appear more masculine than before. In many ways it is difficult to combat this myth, since more often than not the successful female athlete is more muscular than her inactive counterpart. An individual with a high androgen/oestrogen ratio will be more muscular, stronger and faster and likely to be successful. The usual effect is that limb circumference size does not increase substantially since, although muscle size increases, adipose tissue (fat) decreases and, because muscle is denser than fat, the two changes together yield no overall change. It goes almost without saying that the toned quality of firm, trained muscle tissue is also much more attractive than excess adipose tissue.

The inability for the vast majority of women to develop large muscle bulk is generally put down to the female's lack of the male hormone (testosterone), with men usually having up to ten times the testosterone blood levels of females (Hutton, 1980).

Women do not have different types of muscle from men although they may, however, have a tendency to store fat between the muscle bundles to a great extent than males. From a physiological point of view, resistance training programmes and strength training programmes for women do not have to differ from those of men. Studies comparing men and women using identical strength programmes reveal that women gain as much, if not more, strength than do men.

The 2-4 days pre-menstruation require careful planning with thought given to reducing the volume and intensity of elastic strength work placing loads on the sacro-iliac joint. Elastic strength work should be minimised during this phase.

Whilst stressing the fact that male and female strength programmes should be largely similar, the following points should be borne in mind:-

1. It is more than likely that females will have less of a strength background than do their male counterparts, and therefore will have to spend longer 'building the base' before moving on to greater volume and intensity.

2. Many young girls (and parents!!) view weights with great suspicion and it may be advisable to make the first winter's strength work varied, light and interesting. Emphasis should be laid on learning the techniques involved and ensuring that all-round strength is obtained.

3. It has already been highlighted that females lack strength in the arm/shoulder region and therefore, when they commence lifting weights, find it difficult to support the barbell in certain lifts, e.g. cleans, squats, snatches etc. Consideration should therefore be given to initially strengthening the arm/shoulder region so that later more specialised work can be performed.

4. Females after puberty tend to be more 'knock-kneed' than do males which is a mechanical disadvantage. This is due to the fact of having relatively broader hips and the femur therefore runs down to the knee at a more diagonal, less vertical line than the male femur. This lower limb structure can cause knee problems if heavy loads (weights *and* jumping/bounding) are attempted too soon. A careful progression of leg work should be attempted with emphasis placed on all-round development — too rapid a gain in quadricep strength is almost a certain recipe for knee pain.

5. Women have longer spines in relation to their limbs. When lifting weight their spines become a relatively long lever and therefore relatively small poundages can create large overloads. It is advisable to spend some initial work on strengthening and stabilising the muscle that supports the spine before heavy conventional lifting takes place.

Chapter 8

SAFETY AND WEIGHTS

Equipment

1. Always check the equipment to be used. Make sure that all collars are tight and barbells are evenly loaded. Don't assume — always check barbells, stands, benches, pulleys, etc.

2. The lifting floor should be even, firm and non-slip.

3. All equipment used should be soundly constructed and regularly checked and maintained.

4. Footwear must be solid and sturdy for balance and *athlete* protection.

5. Always warm-up before lifting — this should be of a general nature as well as with a barbell (specific).

6. Never train alone — ideally two spotters should be used for each exercise. Spotting is a skill in itself and instruction should be given to potential spotters.

7. Initial lifting should be with moderate weights. Without a grooved-in technique, heavy weights will lead to a poor body position which will probably lead to injury.

8. Correct breathing on all lifts must be taught.

9. Activity must cease whenever sharp pain is experienced.

10. Self-discipline must be developed by the athlete — horseplay must not be permitted.

SAFETY —
Never train alone —
always have a partner
'spotting'

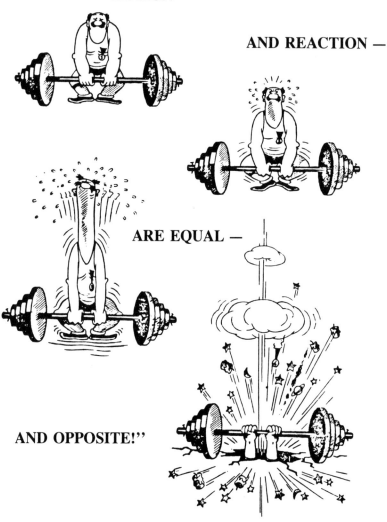

"ACTION —

AND REACTION —

ARE EQUAL —

AND OPPOSITE!"

The floor should be even, **firm** *and non-slip*

TABLE OF PERCENTAGES OF MAXIMUM LIFT

Maximum weight (kg)	35% (kg)	40% (kg)	45% (kg)	50% (kg)	55% (kg)	60% (kg)	65% (kg)	70% (kg)	75% (kg)	80% (kg)	85% (kg)	90% (kg)	95% (kg)
20	7	8	9	10	11	12	13	14	15	16	17	18	19
30	10.5	12	13.5	15	16.5	18	19.5	21	22.5	24	25.5	27	28.5
40	14	16	18	20	22	24	26	28	30	32	34	36	38
50	17.5	20	22.5	25	27.5	30	32.5	35	37.5	40	42.5	45	47.5
60	21	24	27	30	33	36	39	42	45	48	51	54	57
70	24.5	28	31.5	35	38.5	42	45.5	49	52.5	56	59.5	63	66.5
80	28	32	36	40	44	48	52	56	60	64	68	72	76
90	31.5	36	40.5	45	49.5	54	58.5	63	67.5	72	76.5	81	85.5
100	35	40	45	50	55	60	65	70	75	80	85	90	95
110	38.5	44	49.5	55	60.5	66	71.5	77	82.5	88	93.5	99	104.5
120	42	48	54	60	66	72	78	84	90	96	102	108	114
130	45.5	52	58.5	65	71.5	78	84.5	91	97.5	104	110.5	117	123.5
140	49	56	63	70	77	84	91	98	105	112	119	126	133
150	52.5	60	67.5	75	82.5	90	97.5	105	112.5	120	127.5	135	142.5
160	56	64	72	80	88	96	104	112	120	128	136	144	152
170	59.5	68	76.5	85	93.5	102	110.5	119	127.5	136	144.5	153	161.5
180	63	72	81	90	99	108	117	126	135	144	153	162	171
190	66.5	76	85.5	95	104.5	114	123.5	133	142.5	152	161.5	171	180.5
200	70	80	90	100	110	120	130	140	150	160	170	180	190
210	73.5	84	94.5	105	115.5	126	136.5	147	157.5	168	178.5	189	199.5
220	77	88	99	110	121	132	143	154	165	176	187	198	209
230	80.5	92	103.5	115	126.5	138	149.5	161	172.5	184	195.5	207	218.5
240	84	96	108	120	132	144	156	168	180	192	204	216	228
250	87.5	100	112.5	125	137.5	150	162.5	175	187.5	200	212.5	225	237.5
260	91	104	117	130	143	156	169	182	195	208	221	234	247
270	94.5	108	121.5	135	148.5	162	175.5	189	202.5	216	229.5	243	256.5
280	98	112	126	140	154	168	182	196	210	224	238	252	266
290	101.5	116	130.5	145	159.5	174	188.5	203	217.5	232	246.5	261	275.5
300	105	120	135	150	165	180	195	210	225	240	255	270	285
310	108.5	124	139.5	155	170.5	186	201.5	217	232.5	248	263.5	279	294.5
320	112	128	144	160	176	192	208	224	240	256	272	288	304
330	115.5	132	148.5	165	181.5	198	214.5	231	247.5	264	280.5	297	313.5

Repetitions for percentage weights: 100% — 1 repetition; 95% — 2 repetitions; 90% — 4 repetitions; 85% — 6 repetitions; 80% — 8 repetitions; 75% — 10 repetitions.

REFERENCES

BERGER, R.A. Effect of Varied Weight Training Programs on Strength. *Research Quarterly, 33, 168-181,* 1962a.

BERGER, R.A. Optimum Repetitions for the Development of Strength. *Research Quarterly, 33, 334-338,* 1962b.

BERGER, R.A. Comparative Effects of Three Weight Training Programs. *Research Quarterly, 34, 396-398,* 1963a.

BRUNNER, J.A. Untersuchungen über statisches (isometrisches) und dynamisches (isotonisches) Muskeltraining. *Körpererziehung — Swiz,* 1967.

DICK, F.W. Sports Training Principles. *A & C Black,* 1989.

DICK, F.W. Sprints and Relays. *B.A.A.B.,* 1987.

FLECK, S.J. & KRAEMER, W.J. Designing Resistance Training Programs. *Human Kinetics Books, USA,* 1987.

FLECK, S.J., & SCHUTT, R.C. Types of Strength Training. *Clinics in Sports Medicine, 4, 159-168,* 1985.

FOX, E.L. & MATTHEWS, D.K. The Physiological Basis of Physical Education and Athletics. *Saunders (USA),* 1981.

HARRE, D. Trainingslehre. *Sportverlag,* Berlin, 1973.

HETTINGER, R. Physiology of Strength. *Charles C. Thomas,* 1961.

HETTINGER, T. & MULLER, E.A. Muskelleistung und Muskeltraining. *Arbeitsphysiologie, 15, 111-126,* 1953.

HOFFMAN, T., STAUFFER, R.W. & JACKSON, A.S. Sex Differences in Strength. *American Journal of Sports Medicine, 7, 265-267,* 1979.

HUTTON, R.S. & MILLER, D.I. (Eds.). Science Review (pp.149-202) The Franklin Institute, 1980.

JOHNSON, B.L., ADAMCZY, K.J.W., TENNOE, K.O. & STROMME, S.B. A Comparison of Concentric and Eccentric Muscle Training. *Medicine and Science in Sports, 8, 35-38,* 1976.

KOMI, P.V. & BUSKIRK, E.R. Effect of Eccentric and Concentric Muscle Conditioning on Tension and Electrical Activity of Human Muscle. *Ergonomics,* 1972.

LEAR, J. The Powerlifter's Manual. *E.P. Publishing Ltd,* 1982.

MAUGHAN, R.J. Muscle Strength and its Development. *Dunky Wright Memorial Award Lecture,* 1986.

MICHELI, L.J. Overuse Injuries in Children's Sports. *The Orthopedic Clinics of North America, 14, 337-360,* 1983.

MOREHOUSE, C. Development and Maintenance of Isometric Strength of Subjects with Diverse Initial Strengths. *Research Quarterly, 38, 449-456,* 1967.

OLSON, V.L., SCHMIDT, G.L. & JOHNSON, R.C. The Maximum Torque Generated by Eccentric, Isometric and Concentric Contractions of the Hip Abduction Muscles. *Physical Therapy, 52, 148-149,* 1972.

PAYNE, R. & PAYNE, H. The Science of Track and Field Athletics. *Pelham Books, London,* 1981.

SCHMIDTBLEICHER. Strength Training Programs. *European Athletic Coaches Association, Leuven,* 1986.

SEWALL, L. & MICHELI, L.J. Strength Development in Children. *Medicine and Science in Sports and Exercise, 16, 158,* 1984.

TANCRED, B. & G. Weight Training for Sport. *Hodder & Stoughton,* 1984.

VERHOSSHANSKIY, J. Depth Jumping in the Training of Jumpers. *Track Technique, 51: 1618-1619,* 1973.

VIITASALO, V.J., AURA, O., HAKKINEN, K. & KOMI, P.V. Untersuchung von Trainingswirkungen auf die Krafterzeugung und Sprunghöhe. *Leistungssport 11, 278-281,* 1981.

WALDMAN, R. & STULL, G. (1969). Effects of Various Periods of Inactivity on Retention of Newly Acquired Levels of Muscular Endurance. *Research Quarterly, 40, 393-401,* 1967.

WILMORE, J.H. Alterations in Strength, Body Composition, and Anthropometric Measurements consequent to a 10-Week Weight Training Programme. *Medicine and Science in Sports, 6, 133-138,* 1974.

WILMORE, J.H. Physiological Alterations consequent to Circuit Weight Training. *Medicine and Science in Sports, 10, 79-84,* 1978.

WIRHED, R. Athletic Ability & the Anatomy of Motion. *Wolfe Medical Pub. Ltd.,* 1984.

YURACHENKOV, A.I. Deformation of Bones and Joints of Young Sportsmen. *Physical Culture & Sport, Moscow,* 1958.

RECOMMENDED READING

Weight Training and Lifting, by John Lear. Published by A & C Black, London.

The Powerlifter's Manual, by John Lear. Published by EP Publishing Ltd., Wakefield.

Weightlifting (Know the Game series), by BAWLA. Published by A & C Black, London.

Powerlifting — A Scientific Approach, by F.C. Hatfield. Published by Contemporary Books, USA.

Multi-Gym — Basic Instructor's Manual, by Howard Davies. Published by Powersport International Ltd., Wales.

Fitness for Sport, by Rex Hazeldine. Published by Crowood Press, Marlborough.

Designing Resistance Training Programs, by S.J. Fleck/W.J. Kraemer. Published by Human Kinetics Books, USA.

The Complete Guide to Power Training, by F.C. Hatfield. Published by Fitness Systems, USA.

Weight Training for Sport, by B. Tancred/G. Tancred. Published by Hodder & Stoughton, London.

Athletic Ability and the Anatomy of Motion, by Rolf Wirhed. Published by Wolfe Medical Publications Ltd.

The Growing Child in Competitive Sport, edited by Geoff Gleeson. Published by Hodder & Stoughton, London.

The Science of Track & Field Athletics, by H. & R. Payne. Published by Pelham Books, London.

Women's Track & Field Athletics. Published by International Amateur Athletic Federation, London.

Circuit Training, by Manfred Scholich. Published by Sportverlag, Berlin.

Sports Training Principles, by F.W. Dick. Published by A & C Black, London.

Training Theory, by F.W. Dick. Published by British Amateur Athletic Board.